Commentary On Genesis

Volume 2

Discussions In Scripture Series

A Creationist Commentary

By Pastor Steven Waldron

Copyright 2021 by Steven Waldron.

Published 2021.

Printed in the United States of America.

All rights reserved.

No portion of this book may be reproduced, stored in a retrieval system, or transmitted in any form or by any means – electronic, mechanical, photocopy, recording, scanning, or other – except for brief quotations in critical reviews or articles, without the prior written permission of the author.

ISBN 978-1-950647-73-6

Cover image canstockphoto 4243100

Publishing assistance by BookCrafters, Parker, Colorado.
www.bookcrafters.net

An Introduction

THIS IS NOT A MODERN TYPE of Biblical Commentary. Rather, it hearkens back to a time of Scriptural discussions on a popular level from a bygone era. It is an attempt to lift out of Scripture the truths God intended, both in the immediate context and in an applicatory sense. It also does not attempt to answer every question and nuance that Scripture presents. On the essentials it is absolute, such as the Deity of Jesus, monotheism, salvation, holiness, and the character of God. But there are certain ancillary things that very good men disagree on. Paul spoke of days and meats as being some of those issues in Romans 14. According to John 21, the early Church had a rumor that John would not die until Jesus would come back. So, there was latitude on certain things in the early Church. And such there should be today. There is an old saying, "In the essentials unity, in the non-essentials liberty, in all things charity." Now determining what is essential is paramount. God put it like this in Deuteronomy 29:29, "The secret things belong unto the LORD our God: but those things which are revealed belong unto us and to our children for ever, that we may do all the words of this law." Major, essential doctrines will be presented, with other views sometimes offered, and occasionally refuted. Certain issues, such as the identity of the sons of God in Genesis, will be looked at from various viewpoints, but a definitive conclusion may not be proffered. So, we will be discussing Holy Scripture. There is no higher or more important level of discussion that we can have. Oh, that Scripture was on every lip and tongue throughout the world!

Matthew Henry, Thomas Scott, Matthew Poole, Charles Spurgeon, Charles Wesley, and D.L. Moody are among Biblical expositors in times past that would have used a similar style of engagement with Holy Writ. Truth will be presented. However, it may not always be buttressed with the full weight of apologetic argumentation. This present series seeks to be a truthful, honest handling of God's Holy Word in reverence and great care. But it intends on being eminently readable as well. Something to be read enjoyably, as well as a reference work. All evidence for every viewpoint by necessity will not be given. Breadcrumbs may be dropped, handfuls on purpose, to lead to a deeper discovery of truth.

I would be remiss if I did not mention the great mentors and teachers God has so graciously imparted into my life. Dr. Samuel Latta, the great Missionary Evangelist was my Pastor. He died when I was writing this, in the summer of 2019. He will be sorely missed, not just by me, but by the world at large. His passion for Divine Truth is exhilarating. His father, Thomas Latta - Church Planter and Bible expositor nonpareil, had a deep and lasting impact on my life. Sister Ruby Martin of Jackson College of Ministries, and her love of Scripture, was infectious. Pastor Thomas Craft, Dr. David Bernard, Pastor Darrell Johns, Pastor David Reever, Rev. Alan Oggs, Pastor Jonathan Urshan, Pastor Paul Mooney, Pastor Nathaniel Wilson, Pastor Johnny Godair, Pastor Larry Booker, and Rev. O.C. Marler have all sharpened the sword of Scripture in my life in various ways, and for that I am forever grateful. Other ministries and books too countless and laborious to name form a tapestry in my life. The veil of blue, purple, scarlet, cherubim's, and fine twined linen has been sewn warp and woof into my life through them. Without them, and how God used them, my life would in some sense be incomplete. Complete in Jesus yes, but God used them as well. Helpful resources will be mentioned as are deemed appropriate.

The goal is to have a truthful look at each passage of Scripture. Of the making of books there is no end according to Solomon. The world itself could not contain the books that should be written about Jesus. So, it is impossible to flesh each nugget from every jot and tittle of Scripture. Truth, and God's essential revelation is the desired goal. "How can I understand except some man teach me" was a paraphrased cry of the Ethiopian Eunuch. We should study to show ourselves approved unto God, rightly dividing the word of truth.

The Scripture is the mind of God. It has been with God throughout all eternity. He has graciously revealed and preserved it to mankind. Within its pages are life. They testify of Jesus. What greater thing is there to discuss? So, pull up a chair, and with prayerful, reverent, holy awe, let us see how we can apply God's revealed will to our lives, shall we?

I will not follow current grammatical guidelines concerning capitalization of certain sacred subjects. I will capitalize what I feel is sacred, regardless of current conventions of English. That is my prerogative.

Discussions in Scripture 2 – Genesis 7:18 – 12:15

IN THE FIRST INSTALLMENT of Discussions in Scripture, A Young Earth Commentary on Genesis, we went Verse by Verse from the beginning of the present epoch of time, to the middle of Noah's Flood. Somewhere around 1655 years had elapsed in those 178 Verses. We will now go from Genesis 7:18 onward through the beginning of the saga of Abram. The time period herein covered will be from approximately 2349 BC to 1921 BC, or about 428 years.

Genesis 7:18 "And the waters prevailed, and were increased greatly upon the earth; and the ark went upon the face of the waters."

Just by way of background, we are at Sunday, December 7th in the 600th year of Noah's life, or 1656a Anno Mundi (from the creation), 2365 JP (Julian Period), or 2349 BC according to Ussher's wonderful "Annals of the World," meticulously edited by Larry and Marion Pierce, and published by Master Books. This book is highly recommended for its encyclopedic knowledge of the ancient world, both Biblical and secular. Will and Ariel Durant's work "The Story of Civilization" is the only thing I know of that comes remotely close to Ussher.

Technically, we should start at Genesis 7:19, but a little background is in order. The waters prevailed over the earth, because sin had prevailed in the earth. The waters increased greatly upon the earth because sin had increased greatly on earth. The ark goes upon the face of the waters as the Spirit of God did in 1:2. Spirit and water were present at the initial creation. Wood and water are here present. Wood (Cross), water (baptism in Jesus' Name), and Spirit in the New Testament constitute the New Birth experience. Sin is being wiped out, so those in the ark, and the earth itself, can begin anew. In the New Testament, those who are in the ark of salvation (Church) are new creatures in Christ and are looking for new heavens and a new earth wherein dwelleth righteousness.

So the ark is here afloat. The judgment of rain pounds the vessel. But the pitch (atonement – see last book) and wood hold. It rains on the just and unjust alike. But the Church stands.

Genesis 7:19 "And the waters prevailed exceedingly upon the earth; and all the high hills, that were under the whole heaven, were covered."

This was no localized flood. This wasn't the Black Sea inundating the surrounding area. Water seeks its own level. No, this a monumental, worldwide Deluge. All the high hills under the whole heaven. The language precludes localization, and demands earthly universality. The waters were coming from above and up from below. There is still three times more water beneath the earth's surface than above it. Dr. Walt Brown, PhD, MIT postulates that the waters coming from below and exploding upward is the beginning of meteors, comets, and water in our solar system outside of earth's confines. He calculates the force of water coming up in meticulous detail to reach this conclusion. The waters would have blown through the earth's crust at such force, some would have gone through the atmosphere (water and debris).

Outside the ark there was death. Inside the ark was life. There are only two states of man. In Christ, which is life, or in Adam, which is death.

Genesis 7:20 "Fifteen cubits upward did the waters prevail; and the mountains were covered."

We discussed the distinct possibility that the antediluvian cubit was much larger than post Flood cubit. Egyptian, Babylonian, and Hebrew cubits ranged from 18 inches to 26.5 inches. The Semitic cubit was measured from the elbow joint to the hand. Also, many Young Earth Creationists (YEC) feel that mountains per se did not exist until the Flood. Hills, yes, but not mountains. During the extreme upheaval of the floods of the great deep, the hills would have turned into mountains. This would obviously be the case here, as mountains are now formed, if they were not already. As a side note, many feel the New Jerusalem is a mountain. The mountain of the Lord's House and similar imagery. As to whether mountains existed before the Flood, I seem to think they did. Maybe the Flood altered their height, and/or the topography of the earth, but I personally have not seen conclusive evidence that the Flood caused mountains to form. It is possible, however.

Genesis 7:21 "And all flesh died that moved upon the earth, both of fowl, and of cattle, and of beast, and of every creeping thing that creepeth upon the earth, and every man:"

Everything outside the ark died. Adam, as the federal head of the human race, had allowed sin to enter the earth. And death passed upon all men, for all had sinned. But it effected every living thing as well. Life has now passed upon all men, if they will receive it, through Jesus Christ, the Last or Second Adam. Death did not just effect Adam and Eve, it effects every human, and every living thing. Creation groans for the coming, beatific state promised in Scripture.

The Deluge was the beginning of fossilization, geologic columns, and according to many, coal and oil. A beautifully fashioned bell has been found in a very deep coal deposit, confounding scientists. A glimpse of a pre-Flood world, perhaps? There are other Oops Artifacts, worthy of a study by themselves. Items that are discovered, that traditional archaeology says should not exist.

How did plants and trees begin to grow after the Flood, but before the inhabitants of the ark disembarked? It is assumed that somehow sprigs, plants, and trees must have survived the Deluge. How else could the dove and raven never come back, or come back with an olive leaf in its mouth? It is fascinating that the sign of the olive branch is ubiquitous as a sign of peace still to this day, hearkening back to Noah and the Flood.

Genesis 7:22 "All in whose nostrils was the breath of life, of all that was in the dry land, died."

Of course, at least aquatic life and amphibians who could not survive on board the ark would have survived this great cataclysm. With the amount of rain that must have been falling, the vehemence of its rate of descent, I would find it very unlikely that insects could have survived on limbs, branches, and the like. But it is possible, I guess. They say cockroaches would be the likely survivors of a nuclear war. The resilience of nature consistently exceeds expectations in many instances, based on cataclysms experienced around the globe, like Krakatoa, for example.

The survival of fresh and salt water marine life, and its mechanisms, was discussed in the previous volume.

Genesis 2:7 speaks of God breathing into man's nostrils the breath of life. Now that is extinguished. The sheer magnitude of death is stunning to think about. If living things were larger then, the death of everything must have been an exceedingly monumental event. The pre-Flood earth quite possibly had a more universal growing pattern over the face of the globe, based on the contents found in the stomachs of frozen animals in Siberia, and fauna discovered at the poles. Population statisticians show that a human population of over 7 billion existed on earth at the time of the Flood.

This brings us to a so-called problem of the justice of God. How is God just, if women pregnant with babies, babies, and small children died in the Flood, asks the skeptic? The answer proffered is that actually it was an act of mercy on God's part to allow innocence to perish in the Flood. If the children would have lived to the age of accountability, they overwhelmingly, and probably all, would have been wicked, and spent an eternity in hell. Now they are safe in the arms of Jesus. A more philosophical/theological/apologetic treatise could expound on this further. But that is the basics. And as unsatisfying and nuanced as it must be, it really is the best explanation.

Genesis 7:23 "And every living substance was destroyed which was upon the face of the ground, both man, and cattle, and the creeping things, and the fowl of the heaven; and they were destroyed from the earth: and Noah only remained alive, and they that were with him in the ark."

The living substances did not just die, they were destroyed. The earth needed a brand new beginning. This will happen again. Next time it will be by fire.

God never changes His plan based on numbers, else His Word and His Holiness would be violated. It is up to us to correspond to God's plan. We can throw ourselves on the mercy of the Court. But His mercy is to keep us from the Court in the first place. The Court of No Appeal, the Great White Throne Judgment.

So all is dead. Destroyed as it is here. But life was in the ark. Smell and all.

Genesis 7:24 "And the waters prevailed upon the earth an hundred and fifty days."

So for 150 days the water covered everything upon earth. The reason we find shark's teeth on Mt. Everest needs no other reason than this. Five months, destruction lasted. The poor inhabitants of the boat must have had quite a range of emotions. But they were saved to begin anew. The 150 days would lead us to May 6th, 2848 BC.

Chapter 8
The Earth Is Cleansed to Begin Anew

Genesis 8:1 "And God remembered Noah, and every living thing, and all the cattle that was with him in the ark: and God made a wind to pass over the earth, and the waters asswaged;"

Did God forget Noah? The phrase, "And God remembered Noah" merely means He turned His attention to Noah in a particular way. God is Omniscient, He knows all. Of course God was with Noah the entire time. What was life like on the boat those 150 days? 110 of those days with no rain falling, and no great waters from the deep barreling upwards? We could speculate, but no one alive on earth knows. We will one day. But if God did not include it in Holy Writ, it must not be important for us in the current period of time.

Wind begins to evaporate the waters from off the earth (asswaged – from the Proto Indo-European "swad" which means "sweet" or "pleasant"). Things began to get milder in the judgment of the Flood. How fast was the wind? What direction did it blow? We do not know. The wind is obviously a type of the Spirit in Scripture, so we once again have wood (covered with pitch – atonement), water, and wind (Spirit type) saving the world. I have not seen figures on how fast the wind would have had to blow to evaporate that much water. Perhaps fissures drained some of it back downward into the earth. Perhaps more supernatural forces were involved.

Genesis 8:2 "The fountains also of the deep and the windows of heaven were stopped, and the rain from heaven was restrained;"

So, the sources of judgment were stayed. They had fulfilled their course. What had judged the world saved the believer. The type with Jesus' Name baptism cannot be ignored, see 1 Peter 3:21. The discussion of whether salt water was the water of judgment was discussed in Volume One.

Genesis 8:3 "And the waters returned from off the earth continually: and after the end of the hundred and fifty days the waters were abated."

So 40 days of Flood, and 110 days of abatement. A brand new earth. Top soil was replenished with amazing nutritional properties. As we shall see, the curse on growing plants and farming was removed.

Genesis 8:4 "And the ark rested in the seventh month, on the seventeenth day of the month, upon the mountains of Ararat."

Traditional Ararat has 2 mountains, Mt. Ararat and Little Ararat. Many have tried to place the ark other places in the region, finding stone structures possibly ossified, as the ark. The Turkish government's official tourist attraction for the location for the ark was found by Ron Wyatt, and has some interesting attributes to consider. Josh McDowell and others have a spot picked out in Iran as Noah's Ark. The history of Mt. Ararat seems to favor it as in fact its resting place, buried beneath snow and glaciers, and possibly split in two or more pieces.

Berosus the Greek-Babylonian writer mentions the ark around 275 BC, as does Josephus. Many ancient writers soon after Berosus quote him, both BC and AD, about the ark. Josephus mentions many historians in his day who wrote about the ark, including Hieronymus the Egyptian, Mnaseas, and Nicolaus of Damascus, among many others. The Talmud from very ancient times mentions that portions of the ark were being used for idol worship. Even Marco Polo wrote about the ark being on Ararat. The city of Naxuan, or place of descent, is about 17 miles from Ararat. The Epic of Gilgamesh seems to give an excellent description of the area, as Gilgamesh is talking with the Utnapishtim, which closely represents the Biblical Noah. The etymology of the word for Kurds, who inhabit the area, also seems to go back to the words "first" or "descent," describing them as the people in the location of the ark and the inhabitants thereof's descent. It would not have just been Noah and his family, but the descending place of the TRex, Tricoratops, Stegasauourus, the Mammoth's, and such like as well.

Genesis 8:5 "And the waters decreased continually until the tenth month: in the tenth month, on the first day of the month, were the tops of the mountains seen."

Sunday July 19th, 2348 BC, 1,656 years after the creation of the world, the tops of the mountains were seen. The numbers ten and one, mentioned in this Verse may have certain Scriptural significance, but we won't explore that here. I recommend Ed Vallowe or someone else who has written on the significance of numbers in Scripture, such as Bullinger. Gematria, a Jewish understanding of the significance of numbers in the Bible, can possibly be useful, but of course can also be misapplied as well. Do not base doctrines on numbers in Scripture, per se.

Could Noah see the tops of the mountains? As we continue reading, we'll see if there is any possibility that he could at this time while still in the ark. If not, Moses writing as the finger and voice of God some 800 years or so later, could just be writing from God's perspective, as Moses was God's secretary for this portion of Scripture. On whether there were mountains or not until the Flood, we have discussed previously.

Genesis 8:6 "And it came to pass at the end of forty days, that Noah opened the window of the ark which he had made:"

On the 11th day of the 11th month, or August 28th (Friday), Noah opened the window of the ark. Most speculate that this was a window (Genesis 6:16 for specifics) that ran the full length of the ark, or at least a portion protruding from the top. Notice the contrast as well of this window with the windows of judgment (Genesis 7:11). There are so many depictions of the ark, with variations, it is difficult to ascertain exactly what it looked like, outside of Scripture's instruction on building.

What a breath of fresh air that must have been. Many wonder whether the smell of rotting flesh would be palpable. Probably not. Most if not all of the dead flesh would have been crushed under the pressure of the Flood, with much of it becoming fossilized or oil (as some feel). I wonder what the thoughts of Noah and his family were. Everyone dead. The earth left to be populated by the inhabitants of the ark. A fascinating look, at least semi-typologically, of the future repopulating of the earth at the end of this age.

Genesis 8:7 "And he sent forth a raven, which went forth to and fro, until the waters were dried up from off the earth."

According to Leviticus 11:15, the raven was an abomination, so it would have been an unclean bird, if the same designations of clean and unclean were used in this time period as in the Law. Only two ravens would have been on the ark, so for us to have ravens today, it would be imperative for the released one to remain alive. Unclean animals were known to Noah. It did not begin with the Mosaic Law. So this raven did not come back at this time.

Genesis 8:8 "Also he sent forth a dove from him, to see if the waters were abated from off the face of the ground;"

However this window was configured, and it would have had to be constructed a particular way to allow for ventilation in the ark before it was opened, Noah could not see the ground. He was aware he was no longer moving, however. I wonder what the ark stopping on Ararat felt like?

As an aside, notice that Noah was making the decisions. He was the patriarch.

This is the first mention of a dove in Scripture. Mosaic Law does not mention whether it was clean or unclean. The assumption is that it is clean, due to its connation with the Holy Ghost.

Genesis 8:9 "But the dove found no rest for the sole of her foot, and she returned unto him into the ark, for the waters were on the face of the whole earth: then he put forth his hand, and took her, and pulled her in unto him into the ark."

The dove, unlike the raven, returned to Noah. Notice the similarity between this Verse and Genesis 1:2. Also take note that Noah put forth his hand and took the dove. Did the dove land on his raised hand? This would be a significant type of raising our hands to receive the Holy Ghost. But Scripture does not specifically say this. The female dove, we know this one's gender, could have landed on the window's ledge, and Noah grabbed her from there. Or he could have grabbed her in mid-air as she gradually slowed to come to him. The dove returns. How beautiful.

As a side note, some would say the female designation of this dove is equated with feminine characteristics of the Holy Spirit. I see no correlation here.

Genesis 8:10 "And he stayed yet other seven days; and again he sent forth the dove out of the ark;"

Noah was aware of the stationary nature of the ark and wanted to know when it would be safe to disembark, evidently. We are not told if the sending forth of the dove and raven were direct commandments from God, or something that Noah thought of himself.

Genesis 8:11 "And the dove came in to him in the evening; and, lo, in her mouth was an olive leaf pluckt off: so Noah knew that the waters were abated from off the earth."

The olive leaf is still today a symbol of peace. A gentle dove, with its peaceful characteristics, and the olive leaf which produces fruit and beneficial oil, is a beautiful sign of peace. The world had been judged. Peace was now offered.

I am using Ussher's work for the dating of this section. Occasionally, I use Reese. I have noticed in this particular section, there is a 1-2 year discrepancy, something to make you aware of.

How did the olive tree grow? And how did it grow that fast? For a natural explanation, it would have had to be from a sprig that floated for the duration of the Flood, and sprouted and grew in the nutritious soul of the post-Flood world. Or God could have planted it. God could also have given it miraculous growth.

Reese has an excellent breakdown of Noah's timeframe with the Flood. He says Noah was in the ark for a total of 377 days, while mentioning some say 371 days. 7 days of waiting, 40 days of raining, 110 days afloat, 150 days resting while the waters abated, and 70 days for the earth to dry. It is that 70-day period that the small olive shrub could have taken root.

The Great Salt Lake (possibly), fossils in mountains, the Grand Canyon, and other signs point, in many cases, to the remnants of the Flood.

Genesis 8:12 "And he stayed yet other seven days; and sent forth the dove; which returned not again unto him any more."

According to Ussher this would have occurred on the second day of the 12th month, or Friday, September 18th. So the moment has arrived. Time to observe the brave new world. The release of all the animals and insects from the ark. Dr. Walt Brown has cited studies which show that the genetics of mankind extend back to an origin in its present configuration to almost this exact area. Ancient traditions point to this area as well.

Genesis 8:13 "And it came to pass in the six hundredth and first year, in the first month, the first day of the month, the waters were

dried up from off the earth: and Noah removed the covering of the ark, and looked, and, behold, the face of the ground was dry.

Much could be made of the covering mentioned here. It was evidently another layer of sealant to enhance moisture repellence. Observe that Noah at 601 years of age, was still the leader of his family.

Freshwater lakes ostensibly appeared. Mammoth amounts of topsoil was laid down. Mountains were snow-capped, glaciers were formed, an ice age began making the equatorial lands much cooler than today in many instances. Glaciers formed even near the equator on Mount Kenya, for example. The great geologic columns were laid down, and canyons were formed as water receded. The continental separation of Peleg's day was not yet accomplished.

This occurred on Friday October 23rd, 2348 BC. October 23rd, 4004 BC (Sunday), was the first day of creation interestingly enough. Noah (or Noe as it is in the Gospels, a Greek form of his name) no longer had to rely on fowl, he could see the world around him with the removal of the covering. In a future day, God will remove a veil from Israel's eyes, so they can see their Messiah. In Noah's 601st year, on the first day of the first month, the world begins anew. The symbolism couldn't be clearer.

Genesis 8:14 "And in the second month, on the seven and twentieth day of the month, was the earth dried."

Noah and his family remained another 57 days or so in the ark. On Thursday, December 18th, everything leaves the ark.

Genesis 8:15 "And God spake unto Noah, saying,"

In what way did God speak? Audibly, where all could hear, like John 12? Into Noah's spirit? We don't know. God spoke unto Noah in Chapter 6 to build the ark. 100+ years later He spoke again to enter the ark. He then tells Noah a year plus later to leave the ark. Possibly He spoke to Noah often, and it is just not recorded in Scripture. The Spirit of Christ evidently preached through Noah, at least in one interpretation of the Epistles of Peter. Noah heard, and Noah obeyed. Possibly he did not need daily pep talks to remain in obedience. But silence does not mean it did not occur, it simply means it is not recorded. God could have been speaking to Noah, and we have no record.

Genesis 8:16 "Go forth of the ark, thou, and thy wife, and thy sons, and thy sons' wives with thee."

"Leave the ark," was God's Word to Noah. Would there have been a certain amount of fear? The ark was safety. The ark was where provision was. But if there was going to be procreation and renewal of the earth, they had to leave the ark. Go is still the command of God to populate the New Heavens and the New Earth and New Jerusalem, but in a soulwinning realm.

Genesis 8:17 "Bring forth with thee every living thing that is with thee, of all flesh, both of fowl, and of cattle, and of every creeping thing that creepeth upon the earth; that they may breed abundantly in the earth, and be fruitful, and multiply upon the earth."

God shut the door. Did He also open it? Did Noah have to rouse the animals? What were they to eat? If God had brought them this far, He would certainly continue to provide for them. The Genesis 1 command and blessing to be fruitful and multiply was still in effect.

Genesis 8:18 "And Noah went forth, and his sons, and his wife, and his sons' wives with him:"

God told them what to do in verse 16. Here, they obey His command explicitly. There is a great lesson in obedience in this entire saga. Mankind fell due to disobedience. The world has been spared to begin anew with Noah's obedience.

Genesis 8:19 "Every beast, every creeping thing, and every fowl, and whatsoever creepeth upon the earth, after their kinds, went forth out of the ark."

All categories of living creatures leave the ark. How could their legs function after over a year with extremely limited movement? The same God who had the plants live before the sun was created, was still upon the Throne to accomplish this.

Another problem that arises is that man and the animals require oxygen. Plants require Carbon Dioxide. How did this work in the ark when all plant life had been destroyed? Perhaps Noah had plants with him in the ark. But with no sunlight, or at least very little, it would have been difficult for them to grow. Or God did it either supernaturally, or through forces of creation we are not cognizant of. The same problem would present itself with plants growing after the Flood, but before the disembarkment from the ark, or even the opening of the window. But with God all things are possible.

How beautiful that fresh air must have felt in the lungs of man and animal alike! After 377 days or so in a stale ark, the freshness of the air, the brightness of the sun, the shape of the clouds, the shining of the stars, and the beauty of the landscape must have been immense. And if man had never seen snow-capped mountains before, the panorama must have been awe inspiring.

Also notice the different "kinds" of Genesis 1 were still in effect.

Genesis 8:20 "And Noah builded an altar unto the LORD; and took of every clean beast, and of every clean fowl, and offered burnt offerings on the altar."

With the pilcrow (a small flag indicating a new paragraph or thought in the King James Bible) beside the verse number, we see another thought beginning. A paragraph as we would call it in English. God built the Universe. Cain built a city. The rebels will build a tower. Noah built an ark. Here, Noah builds an altar. At the first offering by man in Scripture in Chapter 4, offense occurred and someone died. Noah builds an altar, walking with God like his Great-Grandfather

Enoch. Abraham would become known as the altar builder as future generations examined his life.

As already explained, the differentiation between clean and unclean was designated before this time in an unrecorded part of human history.

Of the dimensions or construction materials of the altar, we know not. It is interesting that this was burnt offerings. Perhaps this was the best way to dispose of the carcasses without the task of burial. Beyond that, I could only speculate at the reason for burnt offerings here.

Genesis 8:21 "And the LORD smelled a sweet savour; and the LORD said in his heart, I will not again curse the ground any more for man's sake; for the imagination of man's heart is evil from his youth; neither will I again smite any more every thing living, as I have done."

Jehovah has a heart? Man is in the image of God (1:26). Since God is a Spirit (John 4:24), this heart must be spiritual. Or it looks forward to the Incarnation. Also, this is a clear example of God communicating with Himself.

God takes no pleasure in the death of the wicked (Ezekiel 18:23). The judgment He had imposed on the sinful world hurt Him at His heart. But this sacrifice of Noah pleased God. We could speculate on whether this was a freewill offering or not, or what would constitute it qualifying as a freewill offering. But the point is, whether it was freewill or simple obedience on Noah's part, He was pleased with the sacrifice.

Notice the ground is either no longer cursed, or the curse upon the ground will not be increased beyond what it already was. The former reading is the consensus view, and one I tentatively hold. Subject to change as further study becomes available!

A modern objection, is what type of God takes pleasure in the killing of innocent animals? Isn't this barbaric? Speaking of which, why did children and animals have to die during the Flood? What evil had they done? Without going into the various justifications and reasonings, let me just say, whatever God does is right. He is the very definition of right and justice. He did it, and it is right. I have written before on the various justifications, and these serve to palliate individuals with questions, sometimes. But as a submitted Christian, I trust God's decisions more than my own. Far more.

The Flood did not change the sinful nature of man. As a matter of fact, this Verse is an excellent prooftext for the sinful nature of the human race. God destroyed the world, partly due to man's sinful heart. It is still there. And another judgement will be forthcoming. Just not by flood.

The next judgement will not destroy every living material thing on earth. So, though it comes by fire, it will be different. Also observe, God takes full responsibility for the judgement He has meted. There are no excuses with God as there is with sinful man.

Genesis 8:22 "While the earth remaineth, seedtime and harvest, and cold and heat, and summer and winter, and day and night shall not cease."

This Verse summarizes the basics of the Noahic Covenant. The Bible nowhere says that summer will be like winter and winter will be like summer in the endtime. Yet, I have met so many people who are convinced that this is in Scripture, even after showing them this Verse. This Verse is a reason why I believe if global warming is occurring, it is or will be very slight, because cold and heat and summer and winter will continue while the earth remains. I do not discount the known phenomenon of heat islands, etc.

In the immediate context, seedtime and harvest is natural agriculture. It could have spiritual connotations of soulwinning as well. And though the days are shortened in the endtime (Revelation 8 and Matthew 24), day and night will continue while this earth remains. We are living on the same earth as in Noah's day. We do look for new heavens and a new earth wherein dwelleth righteousness. The change will be like when one changes a garment.

Chapter 9

Chapter 9 of Genesis introduces us to rainbows and promises. But it also lets us see that sin is still rampant in the world. A question with no answer about the Flood period is, where was satan and the fallen angels during this time? Did they all attack Noah and his family? We really have no way of knowing.

Genesis 9:1 "And God blessed Noah and his sons, and said unto them, Be fruitful, and multiply, and replenish the earth."

Just as God blessed the earth and the things in it in Genesis 1, He now blesses Noah and His sons. The command is the same as in Genesis 1. For those who believe in the Gap Theory, 9:1 is one of their major prooftexts. God uses replenish here, just as He did in Genesis 1. So, if there had been inhabitants and judgment here, why not in Chapter 1 as well? Though this is a valid question, I think the weight of young earth creationism with no Gap Theory is still superior. Words can have different connotations in differing contexts.

With God's blessing comes fruitfulness and multiplication. This command appears to still be in effect. We have to trust God will come back before overcrowding of the earth occurs. The proper use of resources is an issue for feeding and supplying earth's population. Just as Adam and Eve kept the Garden, we are to still be good stewards of the earth. Greed, avarice, and mismanagement, among other failings, prevents so much good to the world.

Genesis 9:2 "And the fear of you and the dread of you shall be upon every beast of the earth, and upon every fowl of the air, upon all that moveth upon the earth, and upon all the fishes of the sea; into your hand are they delivered."

Adam had dominion. This seems to be at least a form of that dominion here presented to Noah and his family. Now did this extend to Noah and his son's offspring? Is it still in effect? Even dinosaurs had a fear of Noah and his family instilled in them by God. As for whether this still holds, I am not sure. It could have just been so the carnivores would allow the nascent human race to survive. Fear and dread are strong terms used here. So, while Man is definitely at the top of the food chain, I am not sure our presence evokes fear and dread. We will see why this is important in the next Verse.

Genesis 9:3 "Every moving thing that liveth shall be meat for you; even as the green herb have I given you all things."

In a seeming change from the Antediluvian world, man will now be an omnivore. Did our teeth change at this time? Our dietary system? Or had we been created in anticipation of this event?

For those who are into nutrition, the significance of green herb should not be missed. Many green foods are beneficial to the human species.

This also means a new occupation will be introduced to the world; hunting for food.

Genesis 9:4 "But flesh with the life thereof, which is the blood thereof, shall ye not eat."

The life of the flesh is in the blood. It is forbidden to eat blood in the Noahic covenant, the Mosaic covenant, and as part of the New Covenant obligations. Leviticus 17:11 says, "For the life of the flesh is in the blood: and I have given it to you upon the altar to make an atonement for your souls: for it is the blood that maketh an atonement for the soul." In the Jewish belief system, at least in part of it, it says the soul is in the blood. For whatever reasons, we are still to abstain from eating blood (Acts 15:20, 29). The JW's get their prohibition against blood transfusions from the references in Acts.

Blood pudding? Rare steaks? Are these permissible? I personally err on the side of caution. I know many conservative Christians who partake in these things, however. Should we all follow kosher meat practices for draining blood from meat? It would be better, for sure.

Genesis 9:5 "And surely your blood of your lives will I require; at the hand of every beast will I require it, and at the hand of man; at the hand of every man's brother will I require the life of man."

God continues His instructions that began in Verse 1. If an animal or human kills a human by the shedding of blood, he must die. The question becomes what of death by strangulation, poisoning, or some other means where blood is not shed. A strictly legalistic interpretation of this Passage would indicate that the death penalty only extends to death with the shedding of blood involved. Or does it? The phrase "the life of man" that closes this Verse may indicate all death by murder should be reciprocated. In Verse 6, the image of God is invoked, further indicating murder by whatever means requires the death penalty. Blood seems to be the point. However, the last phrase here again merely says the life of man. The death penalty appears to be Scriptural for these cases. Any murder unjustified of a human.

It is in these Passages as well we get part of the Noahide Laws of certain groups of Jews. Here, the death penalty for murder is enjoined. Romans 13, Paul seems to give sanction to this view as well. Not necessarily the Noahide Laws in toto, though Romans 2 goes through that concept to an extent. But rather the shedding of blood and murder. Noahide Laws are basically righteous Gentile laws to establish civil government.

Genesis 9:6 "Whoso sheddeth man's blood, by man shall his blood be shed: for in the image of God made he man."

What if blood is shed, but murder does not ensue? What should the punishment be then? It seems that murder is here in view, though retributive civil justice is not necessarily foreign to Scripture.

The reasoning for the death penalty for murder is given because that man is in the image of God. There is possibly a hint or an echo about the sacrifice of Jesus, and His efficacious shedding of blood. But it is a rather opaque reference, if one is indeed meant to be communicated there, at least in my view. Jesus was obviously the perfect image of God. And He shed His Blood.

Genesis 9:7 "And you, be ye fruitful, and multiply; bring forth abundantly in the earth, and multiply therein."

As in Verse 1, and continuing here, this address is not to Noah only, but also his sons. "You" and "ye" are plural terms in the KJV. And Noah and his sons were supposed to teach their wives, one would assume, just as Adam was to teach the Woman. Verse 7 is basically rehashing Verse 1. One could conjecture that the "bring forth abundantly," missing from Verse 1, could connate agriculture, husbandry, etc., but that is uncertain from the context. Most likely it is just for bearing children.

We note also, this was to be done on earth, no mention is made of other planets. Or as some religions teach, in Heaven itself.

Genesis 9:8 "And God spake unto Noah, and to his sons with him, saying,"

Elohim continues to speak with Noah and his sons. The re-emphasis of this fact probably means a different topic is coming into view, or it may be from a later time period that God spoke to them.

It is instructive and fascinating that Noah and his sons were getting instructions on how to begin the post-Deluvian world. God gives His Word. It is up to us to obey it. And Noah and his family had done a great job with obedience.

Genesis 9:9 "And I, behold, I establish my covenant with you, and with your seed after you;"

The entire human race is to be partaker of this covenant. All of us are descendants of Noah. In the next Verse we learn the covenant is not just with humans, however.

A covenant is "berit" in Hebrew, and has the connotation of "cutting" at its root.

Genesis 9:10 "And with every living creature that is with you, of the fowl, of the cattle, and of every beast of the earth with you; from all that go out of the ark, to every beast of the earth."

According to Verse 10, we find that God's Covenant extends to the seed of the living creatures as well. What we find in this covenant seems to eliminate the possibility of a localized Flood once and for all. It is also stunning to realize the diversity of life that came out of the ark, and the immense number of animals.

Genesis 9:11 "And I will establish my covenant with you; neither shall all flesh be cut off any more by the waters of a flood; neither shall there any more be a flood to destroy the earth."

There have been floods in which localized populations of animals and humans were destroyed. Tsunami's, bursting dams, walls of water at hurricanes and typhoons, even river flooding. This promise would have been violated numerous times if the Flood was a localized event. This leads to another issue. Whenever we try to combine the Bible with a modern understanding of science, and compromise plain Biblical truth in the process, it almost always (if not always) ends up bringing contradictions into the Scripture. Best to let Scripture be our guide. So many findings of science, archeology, and history are transitory phenomenon. What one generation accepts as fact, the next disproves. The Word of God is unchangeable. It is that which comports with reality. Truth.

The last phrase of this Verse, if the Flood were merely local, really disproves Scripture. Floods are ubiquitous. One could try to read into Scripture, "not this deep" or something. But it does not say, or imply that. Either the Flood was worldwide, or Scripture is in error. There really is no other option. In the previous volume we looked at the reasons it was universal. These Verses just reinforce that.

Genesis 9:12 "And God said, This is the token of the covenant which I make between me and you and every living creature that is with you, for perpetual generations:"

Covenants normally had tokens, gifts or signs. "The Blood Covenant" by Turnbull, and also another by the same name by Kenyon, explore ancient and Biblical covenants. So there would be a token given by God, even with the animals.

Genesis 9:13 "I do set my bow in the cloud, and it shall be for a token of a covenant between me and the earth."

The rainbow, which evidently did not exist in the cloud before this time, was and is the token of the covenant. The world will never again be destroyed by a Deluge. Every time we see a rainbow, this is God's way of speaking that.

Some have speculated that because it says bow, not rainbow, there is significance there. They would say that the covenant would be a promise to win at spiritual warfare in the heavenlies, by bow, instead of rainbow. God puts the bow there, we supply or pray in the arrows. I do not see any justification for that Scripturally.

There is a rainbow round about the throne in Revelation 4:3. A rainbow is about the head of a mighty angel in Revelation 10:1. We could elucidate speculations about the significance of this, but in the end, it would be just speculation.

Genesis 9:14 "And it shall come to pass, when I bring a cloud over the earth, that the bow shall be seen in the cloud:"

I have seen rainbows while riding in planes. I have seen the end of a rainbow across the street from my home. I have seen double rainbows multiple times. With the dramatic climatic changes during and after the Flood, rainbows were formed for this covenantal purpose.

Rainbows consist of seven colors. Seven seems to be a number of significance to God. Notice as well, it is God Who brings clouds over the earth. Now seems a good time to quote Nahum 1:3.

Nahum 1:3 "The LORD is slow to anger, and great in power, and will not at all acquit the wicked: the LORD hath his way in the whirlwind and in the storm, and the clouds are the dust of his feet."

Genesis 9:15 "And I will remember my covenant, which is between me and you and every living creature of all flesh; and the waters shall no more become a flood to destroy all flesh."

Could God forget, being Omniscient? Why would He need a reminder? Are rainbows like strings tied to His Fingers to help remember? Of course not. God knows all. It may have a connotation of "to bring to the forefront." But of course God knows all, all the time, with or without a rainbow.

Also, fossilization shows all flesh was destroyed during the Flood.

Genesis 9:16 "And the bow shall be in the cloud; and I will look upon it, that I may remember the everlasting covenant between God and every living creature of all flesh that is upon the earth."

God continues speaking. This is one of the longer continuous Passages of Scripture we find God speaking in, though all of the Bible is God speaking in a very real sense.

We see here that the covenant is to be everlasting. The remainder of this Verse is a reiteration of the covenant found in Verse 15. And regardless of how very much it seems that God uses the rainbow to jog His memory, with Omniscience, it is a far more nuanced understanding than that. God needs nothing to jog His memory. It is more of His part of the covenant token. There is no Biblical teaching of Openness Theology, which opines that God is constantly learning and discovering predicated on the free will of His creatures.

Genesis 9:17 "And God said unto Noah, This is the token of the covenant, which I have established between me and all flesh that is upon the earth."

This is the third time the word "token" is used in God's dialogue to Noah and his sons. The word "token" is found 14 times in Scripture, including four times in the NT. A synonym for token would be sign. It means it is established

Genesis 9:18 "And the sons of Noah, that went forth of the ark, were Shem, and Ham, and Japheth: and Ham is the father of Canaan."

The three sons of Noah are not mentioned from oldest to youngest here. Canaan is mentioned, evidently because of the part he is to play in the immediate narrative, and his descendants' role throughout the remainder of the Old Testament. The theory that Ham's wife was impregnated by a Nephilim before the Flood, and gave birth during the Flood, has no Biblical credence other than speculation. Some say this had to be so because giants are found on this side of the Flood, as well. But there are other means of causality that are just as plausible, if not more so.

Genesis 9:19 "These are the three sons of Noah: and of them was the whole earth overspread."

From these three came every famous personage of post-Flood history. Socrates, Julius Caesar, the Emperors of China, Napoleon, David, Moses, Abraham, Sarai, Rebecca, Rachel, Deborah, and the rest of the human race came from this lineage. Chapter 10 will give us the details of the 70 Nations of the world.

Now of course, this overspreading took time. How much time is a matter of conjecture. If the receding Flood waters turned into an ice age, as the evidence shows, it could have been quicker than thought possible. The ice would have been taking up a fairly large chunk of the earth's surface.

Genesis 9:20 "And Noah began to be an husbandman, and he planted a vineyard:"

Reese lists the ages of Noah's sons at the time of disembarkment from the ark as Japheth 101, Shem 99, and Ham 97. He then puts the next several Verses six years later, with Ham being 103.

In the first creation, Adam was to keep a garden. In this new creation, so to speak, Noah becomes a husbandman, or a tiller of the ground. In Eden, God planted everything. And of course, with the olive leaf in the dove's mouth, something, whether natural or supernatural, must have occurred in replanting the botanical world. But Noah planted the vineyard. How plant life overspread the post-Flood world, is not specifically known. We could name certain mechanisms that would have accomplished it, and it may have been a conglomeration of some or all of them, or it could have been something entirely different.

It is fascinating that the Mediterranean region is known for olives and grapes to this day. Olive leaves, by the way, are considered to be a potent antiviral.

Genesis 9:21 "And he drank of the wine, and was drunken; and he was uncovered within his tent."

Many, if not most, expositors of Scripture attempt to ameliorate Noah's drunkenness here. They say that with the atmospheric changes after the Flood, fermentation would have been heretofore unknown, or it would have occurred through differing mechanisms. So, it was an accidental drunkenness. This could be true. But the Scripture is silent. We do know Noah had the fortitude to withstand the entire sin-soaked world to save his family and serve God. At the same time, the greatest of men have a sin that does so easily beset them. The fallen human heart has sin residing in it. This occurred before the Holy Ghost's indwelling that occurs at the New Birth.

This is the first of many prohibitions against alcohol and drunkenness in Scripture. The pamphlet, "75 Reasons the Bible Says You Should Not Drink Alcohol," or some similar title, by Spirit of Freedom Ministries in Louisiana is an excellent source on this subject.

But there are a host of other items that are enlightening on the subject also.

How Noah got naked we are not told. To this day, drunkenness and nakedness are vices of mankind, and so often go together. What follows here is one of the most controversial portions of Scripture in Holy Writ.

Genesis 9:22 "And Ham, the father of Canaan, saw the nakedness of his father, and told his two brethren without."

Ham sees his father's nakedness, and tells Shem and Japheth. But it is randomly mentioned, seemingly, that Ham is the father of Canaan. What bearing does this have on the narrative? Was Canaan the firstborn of all the children after the Flood? Regardless, Canaan will play a part in the upcoming drama.

Was modesty such a big issue, that to look upon a close relative of the same sex would be the cause of a perpetual curse? Let's continue to examine and unpack this fascinating story.

Genesis 9:23 "And Shem and Japheth took a garment, and laid it upon both their shoulders, and went backward, and covered the nakedness of their father; and their faces were backward, and they saw not their father's nakedness."

It does seem the act of gazing was sufficient to bring about the forthcoming curse. Shem and Japheth did not look on their father's nakedness. They averted their eyes.

Did Ham make fun of his father? Was something more than looking involved? Let's continue.

Genesis 9:24 "And Noah awoke from his wine, and knew what his younger son had done unto him."

Further information seemingly enters the Text. Noah knows his younger son Ham had done something to him. Waking up naked with a blanket or garment over you, wouldn't necessitate something being done to the person. Something had happened, quite possibly beyond gazing and looking. The Scripture is quite opaque here. I don't think anything definitive beyond the looking can be established, only speculated. The question remains, how would Noah realize it was Ham who had done whatever act was done? Had they been drinking together? Was there a pattern of malfeasance? Did the other sons, or Noah's grandson tell him? We don't know. And in the grand scheme of things, if God chose not to tell us, we do not need to know.

Genesis 9:25 "And he said, Cursed be Canaan; a servant of servants shall he be unto his brethren."

God cursed the serpent in Genesis 3:14, and the ground in 3:17. Cain was cursed from the earth in 4:11. God had done that cursing. Now Noah, in the image of God, curses Canaan. Had Canaan partaken in whatever Ham had done?

There is no Hamitic Curse. This was a false teaching that was used to keep Blacks in slavery and oppression. The curse was not on Ham, it was on Canaan. He was to be a servant of servants to his brethren. This seems to refer to Shem, Japheth, their offspring, and Ham's other offspring. More specifics come in Verse 26. Was it to be in perpetuity?

Genesis 9:26 "And he said, Blessed be the LORD God of Shem; and Canaan shall be his servant."

The Jehovah Elohim of Shem would be blessed. Out of Shem's lineage would come Abraham and the Messiah, Jesus. Canaan will be Shem's servant.

Can mankind still curse people effectually? Our words are powerful. But this may have been more prophetic in nature. Pronouncing rather than enacting a curse. Much like Paul to Bar-Jesus (Elymas) in Acts 13.

Genesis 9:27 "God shall enlarge Japheth, and he shall dwell in the tents of Shem; and Canaan shall be his servant."

Many extend this out to their descendants. Japheth would be enlarged. He would have a large land area. But Shem would have the money, or own the tents. Some issues with that are obvious. It could just mean Shem would be a tent maker.

Genesis 9:28 "And Noah lived after the flood three hundred and fifty years."

350 years is an enormous amount of time. It is five times the three score and ten lifespan. The Sumerian King List speaks of long ages for pre-Flood man. When you overlap Noah's life after the Flood, you get very close to the birth of Abraham. Noah died around 1998 BC and Abram was born around 1996 BC. A few chronologies actually have Noah and Abram overlapping.

Noah and his family are unique to the human race in being able to see what life was like before and after the Flood. They are like Adam and Eve in that respect, Adam and Eve being able to know what pre-Fall and post-Fall life was like. We will see the lifespan of mankind gradually diminish as we continue through Scripture, coalescing around the aforementioned threescore and ten. Life for much of human history has been nasty, brutish, and short, as Thomas Hobbes said.

Genesis 9:29 "And all the days of Noah were nine hundred and fifty years: and he died."

As before the Flood, so after. "And he died" was a determining feature of pre-flood man, as seen in Chapter 5. Noah follows. It is appointed unto man once to die, and after that, the judgment.

Noah would live long enough to see the Tower of Babel and its rebellion, and live to see the world to begin to be repopulated. Truly God had blessed living things to be fruitful and multiply. He also saw the earth divided in Peleg's day.

Genesis 10

I DON'T NECESSARILY do an introduction to each Chapter. I do feel one is in order here. According to Jewish reckoning, there are 70 Nations listed in Chapter 10. I was just reading something from a Jewish Author the other day, who mentioned the 70 Nations. He mentioned it as being part of their understanding of the world even to this day, at least in his instance. Many of the names and people groups will be found throughout Scripture, and in a few cases, even to the present time. The best reckoning from a Bible honoring perspective of this portion of Scripture I have ever read is by Barry Bietzel. He did the "Moody Bible Atlas," the "Biblica Bible Atlas" I believe, and the maps for new "Schuyler Bibles." He is excellent in my view.

Reese, in his Study Bible, gives some interesting information concerning Chapter 10. The following is a summation of some of his statements:

Of the 70 Nations, 26 came from Shem, 30 from Ham, and 14 from Japheth. Shem's descendants settled from the Mediterranean to the Indian Ocean, including Persia (Elam), Assyria (Asshur), Chaldea (Arphaxad), Asia Minor (Lud), and Syria (Aram). Joktan settled Arabia, meaning Shemites (Semites) are Arabians as well as Jews. Shem had five sons, Ham four, and Japheth seven. Ham's offspring went to Ethiopia (Cush), Egypt (Mizraim, which is still the Hebrew word for Egypt), Canaan, and Phoenicia/Libya/North Africa (Put). Japheth, who Dr. Bill Cooper in tracing European lineages, says his name is the original corruption of Jupiter (that part is not from

Reese). Japheth's descendants settled primarily in or near Europe and western Asia. Scythians, Greeks (Ionians), Slavs, Medes, Cimmerians, Turks, Thracians, as well as others.

"After the Flood," a book by Bill Cooper is an exhaustive resource with fascinating harmonizations between the various ancient genealogies, especially of Europe. He is masterful in showing how they all agree.

Genesis 10:1 "Now these are the generations of the sons of Noah, Shem, Ham, and Japheth: and unto them were sons born after the flood."

"These are the generations," seem to be a natural division of the Book of Genesis, being used often, as discussed in the previous volume. Again, we take note that Noah's sons' names are not in correlation to their age. We also see that sons were born after the Flood, not during it.

Genesis 10:2 "The sons of Japheth; Gomer, and Magog, and Madai, and Javan, and Tubal, and Meshech, and Tiras."

While not listed in birth order in Verse 1, the eldest does begin the genealogy here. There is some dispute among some of the names and what geographical area they occupied. I will give some prominent possibilities and probabilities in some cases, but many times nothing definitive.

Many feel Gomer gave rise to the etymology of Germany. Magog, the Great Wall of China was known as the wall of Magog. It was to keep Magog out, so somewhere in what is currently known as Russia could very well be Magog. Chuck Missler wrote what I feel is the definitive work identifying Magog with Russia, in his book "The Coming Magog Invasion." Madai, many would say, are the Medes. Kurds still have traditions concerning Madai. Some say Crete. "Javan" is what the Hebrews called Greece. The name is cognate with "Ionian." Meschech, many feel this is the root of the word "Moscow." A whole host of possibilities have been postulated, almost all of them hundreds of miles North of Israel. "Tiras" indicates Thracians, Estrucans, or the Teresh Sea People.

These would all be the Grandsons of Noah. If daughters were involved, much like Chapter 5, we are not told. But the name normally came from the man, as in Genesis 5:2.

Genesis 10:3 "And the sons of Gomer; Ashkenaz, and Riphath, and Togarmah."

Togarmah is seen by many as being etymologically connected with Turkey, Anatolians or Khazars. Ashkenaz, Jews from Eastern Europe are still known as "Ashkenazi." Riphath, could be Celts, Sauromatians, or from the Carpathian Mountains. Very opaque lineage. These would be Noah and his wife's great-grandsons.

Genesis 10:4 "And the sons of Javan; Elishah, and Tarshish, Kittim, and Dodanim."

More great-grandsons of Noah are in view. Elishah founded Cyprus, the Aeolians, or a Germanic tribe? Tarshish, Gibralter, Britain, or even America are among the possibilities. In Upper Michigan, an ancient Phoenician mine has been found. The Phoenicians said Tarshish was a source of important metals. Kittim, Cyprus or Rome. Dodanim, Rhodes is a likely identification.

Before we go any further, I would like to say I very much should give the meaning of the various names, and not just the place where their descendants eventually inhabited or founded. We find in the next Chapter, that they stayed together for quite some time. As far as the meaning of the names, as much as they are known, will be in a Bible names book like "Jackson's" (the classic) or Judson Cornwall, or often in a good Bible Dictionary or Encyclopedia. So, for the moment, I think we will just concentrate on place of settlement, and not on the meaning of the names, though that is fascinating of itself. I will try to give some definitions as we progress, however. It gives insight into what people were thinking at a point in time by the names they were assigning, oftentimes.

Genesis 10:5 "By these were the isles of the Gentiles divided in their lands; every one after his tongue, after their families, in their nations."

If in the preceding Verses personages are in view, and not Countries, then Javan should be seen to have offspring settling near the Sea. Notice that this has reference after the Tower of Babel episode of Chapter 11. They had a particular tongue (language), and they also became Nations. Nations began during this time period post-Flood.

Genesis 10:6 "And the sons of Ham; Cush, and Mizraim, and Phut, and Canaan."

The Cushite line will play a large role in Chapter 11. Bill Cooper has much historical research on Cush's possible impact on the world. Cush settled somewhere around Ethiopia. Eastern African languages are still designated Cushitic languages. His name appears in Egypt in the 21st Century BC. "Mizraim" is of course the Hebrew word for Egypt. Phut, parts of Egypt, Ethiopia, or Phoenicia. Canaan, would be basically the parameters of modern Israel. And at least some of the Phoenicians, it is thought, later settled in Carthage. The term, "Punic," those of Carthage, is a derivative of Canaan.

Genesis 10:7 "And the sons of Cush; Seba, and Havilah, and Sabtah, and Raamah, and Sabtecha: and the sons of Raamah; Sheba, and Dedan."

Great-grandsons of Noah are seen here. Seba, probably northeastern Africa. Some connect it with Meroe, an island of Ethiopia. It is mentioned elsewhere in the Old Testament. Havilah is mentioned in Genesis 2, and twice here in Genesis 10 (two different people). Havilah is thought to be Arabia or Somalia. Sabtah, southern Arabia, most likely. Raamah, Yemen or SW Arabia are possibilities, or even the Sabeans. Sabtecha, Persian Gulf, or a Province of Ethiopia, whose name has been discovered on Egyptian monuments.

We are now introduced to great-great-grandsons, thru Raamah,

Sheba and Dedan. Sheba and Dedan are often listed together in Scripture. Sheba means "seven," or "an oath." The Queen of Sheba and Bathsheba are rather famous personages of Scripture with whom the name is found, as are Jehosheba, and Beersheba (place name). Yemen or Ethiopia.

Dedan means "friendship," "breast," "judge," "slowly." NW coast of the Persian Gulf.

I must mention here that Josephus lists his understanding of these various places. Being Jewish in the 1st Century AD, at least some credence and deference should be given to his identifications.

Genesis 10:8 "And Cush begat Nimrod: he began to be a mighty one in the earth."

A great-grandson of Noah, Nimrod, is extremely famous both within and outside the Bible. Nimrod is mentioned four times in Scripture. His name means "Rebel" or "Rebellion." As we journey through the next two chapters, it will become apparent why Nimrod has such an outsized influence on post-Flood history.

Being a mighty one in the earth means evidently that he began to exercise influence over others. Many have said Nimrod married Semiramis, was killed somehow, and Semiramis birthed a son, Tammuz, who was to be the reincarnation of Nimrod. All were to be worshipped, and most ancient, false religions could trace their origins back to the worship of this triad. There may be some evidence for this historically and archaeologically, but it is not conclusive. Jewish and Islamic traditions have Abraham and Nimrod meeting, sometimes confrontationally. Other traditions have Nimrod discerning through astrology that a defender of monotheism was to be born in Abram, and he ordered the babies slaughtered to stop this. Most assume Nimrod led the rebellion of the Tower of Babel in Chapter 11, and the implication is clearly there.

A word about Cush. There are various postulations about his identity in antiquity. I am not sure anything concrete has been identified about him. The same could be said for Nimrod as well, including identifying him with Sargon of Akkad. Again, interesting, but not conclusive.

Genesis 10:9 "He was a mighty hunter before the LORD: wherefore it is said, Even as Nimrod the mighty hunter before the LORD."

A few observations are in order. God is a Shepherd. Moses, David, Abraham, Jesus (John 10) are referred to as Shepherds. Nimrod was a mighty hunter. Mankind was probably vegetarian until after the Flood. Nimrod was leading the vanguard in the new way of eating, flesh. Also, it is speculated that he hunted men, not for food, but for domination. His popularity in the ancient world was such, that a saying was built around his reputation. Ancient statues and glyphs from this period show a large human who would hold a lion in an arm as a pet. Others would show a King riding in a chariot hunting lions. Nimrod seems to have been a high type A personality, a real alpha male. And the speculation is so much more.

Genesis 10:10 "And the beginning of his kingdom was Babel, and Erech, and Accad, and Calneh, in the land of Shinar."

Students of Mesopotamian history will immediately recognize names in this Verse. Babel, Erech (Uruk), Accad (Akkad), and Calneh. Babel, of course, needs no introduction and is the likely place of Babylon (there is some dispute about this, however). The Akkadian (Accad) language and culture is very famous in the Ancient Near East (ANE). Uruk (Erech) is located east of the Euphrates River, and is the city of the legendary King Gilgamesh. Many associate Calheh with Nippur, and it is not to be confused with the Calneh used over a millennia later in Scripture.

Shinar is the general area of Mesopotamia. Some see etymological affinities with Sumer. Nimrod must have been amazingly industrious to found these cities and principalities we know of from the Bible and archaeology. Notice here the word "kingdom." To have a kingdom, you must have a king. That would be Nimrod. It was his kingdom.

He could be said to be the founder of post-Flood Monarchial earthly government. Some legends say the Annunaki, or demons, taught him this. Again, that is pure speculation. But his power, authority, and kingdom had to be immense. To keep his kingdom in line, Nimrod would have to use force, fear, and superstition, one would assume. A kingdom that size would not maintain order by itself. Organization must have been present. We know they were incredibly advanced in building, astronomy, and metallurgy, among other things (such as trigonometry) because of multiple archaeological discoveries.

Genesis 10:11 "Out of that land went forth Asshur, and builded Nineveh, and the city Rehoboth, and Calah,"

We are now presented with the figure of Asshur, who continued Nimrod's kingdom building. In researching Asshur, there seems to be some confusion. Some feel Asshur is a city, and others regard him correctly as a person. Those who feel Asshur is a city name, would say that Nimrod also built the other cities mentioned in this Verse. I think the linguistic evidence indicates Asshur was a person. Later, another Asshur is a son of Shem. It seems that many times the two are conflated. "Asshur" is the Hebrew word for "Assyria," basically. So out of Nimrod's kingdom went forth Ashhur and builded. Possibly he was Nimrod's successor or a trusted partner. Josephus, and the Jubilee's manuscript find in the Dead Sea Scrolls, both seem to buttress the claim that Asshur was a person. Some feel he was deified, and hence the name being applied to the future peoples of Assyria.

Asshur built Nineveh, of who so much of the Old Testament is centered around. It is currently located in the eastern half of Mosul Iraq, on the eastern shore of the Tigris River. It was the largest city in the world for quite some time in the seventh century BC. The name, though obscure, seems to refer either to house of fish, or the name of a fish goddess. Hislop expounds on this.

Rehoboth is the name of at least three separate towns in Scripture. It basically means "city of streets," or something close to that. Little is known of the location mentioned here in Verse 11.

Calah seems to be ancient Nimrud, located about 30 miles south of Nineveh/Mosul in the Nineveh plains. The seemingly obvious connection between the name Nimrud and Nimrod, and the major part it played in the later Assyrian empire, shows the deep importance of the city.

Genesis 10:12 "And Resen between Nineveh and Calah: the same is a great city."

Resen, also built by Asshur, should be about 15 miles from both Nineveh and Calah. Its remains have not been definitely identified. It could be buried beneath the sands, or it could have faced a brick by brick removal, which was not uncommon in BC warfare, or even AD times. It must have been something spectacular based on the description in this Verse.

Genesis 10:13 "And Mizraim begat Ludim, and Anamim, and Lehabim, and Naphtuhim,"

Before we get into the regular identifying of the personages and progeny here, an observation is in order. Often times the mistaken assumption is made that "im" at the end of a word such as Elohim is a plurality of persons. Yet here we have five individuals with the "im" ending, yet no one would seriously argue that these are anything other than individuals. So Elohim does not necessitate a plurality of persons.

Mizraim, or Egypt, is the son of Ham, and grandson of Noah. Ludim seems to be the progenitor of the Libyans in North Africa or Lydians in Western Turkey. Anamim seems to be associated with Egypt. Lehabim seems once again to be connected with Libyans in North Africa. Naphtuhim seems to be associated with a region of Egypt.

Genesis 10:14 "And Pathrusim, and Casluhim, (out of whom came Philistim,) and Caphtorim."

Mizraim had seven children. The list is continued here in Verse 14.

Pathrusim indicates Pathros in Upper Egypt, according to many. Casluhim refers to people from a particular part of Egypt, and is attested to in ancient literature. His name possibly means "fool. "Philistim evidently came from Casluhim, and are known later in Scripture as the vaunted Philistines, according to most authorities. The Philistines were a branch of the Phoenicians. Some feel Philistim came from Caphtorim. This is a disputed portion of Scripture, but I stick with the Casluhim interpretation.

Caphtorim: "Caphtor" is the Hebrew name for the island of Crete, and possibly the entire Aegean region. Some feel that Casluhim was the father of both Philistim and Caphtorim, while others think Caphtorim was a separate son of Mizraim. Many ancient inscriptions mention Caphtor.

I did want to clarify something. Sometimes I will treat a name as an individual, and sometimes as a people group or Nation. The Bible in this portion seems to have both meanings usually in view.

Genesis 10:15 "And Canaan begat Sidon his firstborn, and Heth,"

Canaan means "low," or "subjugated," or possibly "the color purple." He is the cursed one from Chapter 9. Sidon may mean "hunting or fishing place." It is still located about 25 miles north of Tyre and 25 miles south of Beirut. Heth gave rise to the Hethites (Hittites). The Hittites figure prominently in Scripture. They were considered to be fictitious and a proof of the mythological character of Scripture until its capital Boghazkoy was discovered in the 19th century. Heth may mean "terror," or "dread." The children of Heth would later sell Machpelah to Abraham for a burial cave in Genesis 23.

Genesis 10:16 "And the Jebusite, and the Amorite, and the Girgasite,"

Canaan had 11 children. This continues the list. The Jebusite were inhabitants of Jebus, or Jerusalem (1 Chronicles 11:4), hence extremely valuable, historically. Jerusalem is not mentioned until Joshua 10:1, though Salem is mentioned in Genesis 14:18. Jerusalem must have had a duel designation for a time, or part of the city was known as, Jebus. This is congruent with Canaanite historiography however, with the location of the Canaanites primarily being the Levant (Israel).

The Amorite are known as Amurru in ancient Sumerian and Akkadian texts, and were said to have dwelt in Canaan, then Syria, then Mesopotamia, beginning about 2400 BC according to secular scholarship, comporting quite nicely with the basics of Scripture. The Girgasites were dwellers in Canaan according to several Biblical passages, and their name evidently means "dwellers in the clay-like soil."

Genesis 10:17 "And the Hivite, and the Arkite, and the Sinite,"

Hivites were dwellers of Northern Israel and Southern Lebanon. The name means "tent dweller" or "dweller in a tent city," possibly indicating nomadic tendencies. The Arkites were possibly located in Northern Lebanon near the seacoast. During Roman times its name was Caesarea, currently referred to as Arqa (similar to Arkite). It is mentioned in the Amarna Letters and various Assyrian documents as well. Sinite possibly refers to a region in Northern Lebanon, with at least four cites with this designation as a root. Some even speculate that parts of China were eventually inhabited by some of the Sinites. The last phrase of Verse 18 may indicate this possibility.

Often in Chapter 10, I use phrases of possibility, that are not emphatic. This is the most accurate stance to take, unless a place has been positively identified. A few times I will mention an alternate interpretation to what I think is clear. I do this just in case the reader confronts this somewhere.

Genesis 10:18 "And the Arvadite, and the Zemarite, and the Hamathite: and afterward were the families of the Canaanites spread abroad."

The Arvadites descended from Arvad, and dwelt on the only island of Syria, which bore the name Arvad. It means "I shall break loose." It is currently known as Ruad Island. Prolific seafarers, they were recognized throughout history for their amazing naval capabilities. They possibly founded or settled, at least in part, Burma in SE Asia. The Zemarites settled at Sumra at the foot of the western Lebanon mountains. In the Amarna Tablets, they are a very important Phoenician city, circa 1400 BC. Zemar, of course would almost certainly be the son of Canaan's name. The Hamathite were descendants of Hamath (fortress). They settled on the Orontes River, and were known in antiquity. The current name of the city is still Hamath. Their descendants, at least in part, migrated toward Greece and Macedonia. The Greeks and The Romans knew Hamath as Epiphaniea. Hamath may have an etymological root connected with Ham.

It is worth re-mentioning that the Canannites were not stagnant, but gradually spread over a wide area outward from Israel and Lebanon and their immediate vicinities.

Genesis 10:19 "And the border of the Canaanites was from Sidon, as thou comest to Gerar, unto Gaza; as thou goest, unto Sodom, and Gomorrah, and Admah, and Zeboim, even unto Lasha."

This shows us that the Canaanites covered most of what we would call Israel, into Lebanon. And of course, based on 10:18b, they would expand from there. This Verse also shows us that this is referring to the time the cities of the Plain were still in existence, before the judgment of God in Genesis 19, somewhere around 1897 BC.

Genesis 10:20 "These are the sons of Ham, after their families, after their tongues, in their countries, and in their nations."

So beginning in Verse 6, and concluding here, we have the sons of Ham. The mention of tongues indicates that this goes past the dispersal at Babel in Chapter 11, since all were of one language before that. A Country is a geographical border and Nations are unified somewhat culturally. Families, and incredible extended families, come first in the Verse. No birth control, a command to be fruitful and multiply, DNA closer to the time period of Eden, so not as much degradation, would have led to a very rapid increase of population. Population statisticians say beginning at the Flood, the world's population currently should be about 7.8 billion people. Much older than that, the world could not fit the number of people on the planet.

We also see here that the designations listed in this Chapter go from individuals to people groups.

Genesis 10:21 "Unto Shem also, the father of all the children of Eber, the brother of Japheth the elder, even to him were children born."

Eber is a fascinating study. Many feel that "Eber" is the root of the word for Hebrew. We here are informed that Japheth is the elder. Notice the special attention given to the children of Eber. Shem, again, is where we get the term Semitic.

Genesis 10:22 "The children of Shem; Elam, and Asshur, and Arphaxad, and Lud, and Aram.

The children of Shem explode upon the scene in this Passage. Elam, which is Persia. Several other Biblical personages are referred to as Elam as well. Asshur, many people feel, is the same person as mentioned in Verse 11. I think they are 2 different people, or at least that is how it seems in the natural reading of the Text. The first Asshur seemed to be associated with Hamites, this one, one of the five sons of Shem. But it is possible they are referring to the same individual. Since Asshur appears in Verse 11 with no backstory, the assumption could be made that it was obviously referring to this one. Either way, Asshur refers to Assyria, but just as there are six Ur's in the Ancient Near East (ANE), duplicate names are not uncommon.

Arphaxad is associated with the founding of Ur of the Chaldees by many. He is the 12th of names mentioned in Luke 3:36-38 from Adam to Terah. Lud is often associated with the Lydian's in Turkey. Aram means "highland," and is usually associated with the Arameans of Northern Syria. Aramean is even synonymous with Syria, according to some. It is quite probable this is where the term "Aramaic" comes from, a closely related semitic language to Hebrew. The Ebla Tablets of the third millennium BC and other ancient inscriptions and references refer to Aram.

Genesis 10:23 "And the children of Aram; Uz, and Hul, and Gether, and Mash."

Job was from the land of Uz (Job 1:1). Those who argue for a very early date for Job would seem to have this on their side, though another Uz is mentioned in Genesis 36:28. Either way, it would still be pre-Mosaic. Uz may mean "fertile land," but where this great grandson of Noah settled is not definitely known. Hul, another of the four sons of Aram, founded Armenia, according to Josephus. Hul means "circle" or "writhing." Gether, the third son, is credited with being the founder of the Bactrians by Josephus. Bactria is in NE Iran, and into the three "stan" area, and is seen in Iranian folklore as one of 16 perfect lands created by ahura mazda. Mash is translated as "Meshech" in 1 Chronicles 1:17. He possibly inhabited some Northern part of Mesopotamia.

Genesis 10:24 "And Arphaxad begat Salah; and Salah begat Eber."

In this Passage, it appears Arphaxad only had one son, or at least only one recorded here. His name was Salah. Salah is in Israel's lineage, and the Messiah's. In Genesis 11:12 Salah was born when Arphaxad was 35 years old, in 2311 BC. Arphaxad was born to Shem two years after the Flood, when Shem was 100, according to Genesis 11:10. Now, of course, the mysterious Cainan of Luke 3:36 is interesting to briefly examine here. In the Lukan Passage, it says Cainan is Salah's father. This leads people to accept the Septuagint, which inserts Cainan, and also argue for gaps in the Genesis genealogies, since Cainan is not mentioned. It could be something as simple as Cainan died at birth, or in the womb. Possibly he had relations with Arphaxad's unnamed wife. Regardless, Cainan is not mentioned here or in Chapter 11, which is very specific in the lineage, especially since it concerns the Messiah. That Cainan was a real person, we have no doubt. What role he played in begetting Salah is only speculation. There is no error in the Text. It is like the term "son" in regnal succession. Sometimes the son is literal, sometimes merely regnal succession is meant. Lot is Abram's nephew, but called a brother. Cainan's role is something to be deduced. Luke included it, so it is somehow important. Sometimes that is all we know.

Deuteronomy 29:29 reads, "The secret things belong unto the LORD our God: but those things which are revealed belong unto us and to our children for ever, that we may do all the words of this law."

Salah may mean "branch" or "javelin," and his name may give more hints on the identity of Cainan. Eber is thought by many to be the root of the word "Hebrew." Eber means "crossing over," Hebrew means "crossing the river," as when Abram crossed the river to get to the Promised Land. This is why many assume Eber is the root word for "Hebrew." In Chapter 11, I will try to get into more specifics with the dates, from Ussher in most if not all cases, of this line.

Genesis 10:25 "And unto Eber were born two sons: the name of one was Peleg; for in his days was the earth divided; and his brother's name was Joktan."

After a couple of generations of the genealogies recording having only one son, Eber has two, Peleg and Joktan. How was the earth divided? Some say that was just the division at Babel, and that may be what it is referring to. Others say this is the breakup of Pangea, all Continents then being together, but the way the Earth's crust is, that may be unlikely. Walt Brown has developed a very plausible model of land bridges becoming gradually or suddenly filled with water after the Flood, thus separating the continents. Some say this occurred 105 years or so after the Flood. I would refer you to Morris, Ussher, Brown, and Jones for a detailed explanation of that. Peleg means "brook," and his settlement is uncertain.

Joktan has 13 sons recorded through Verse 30. Joktan according to the Jewish Encyclopedia was the progenitor of 13 Arab tribes. Joktan means "he will be small."

Genesis 10:26 "And Joktan begat Almodad, and Sheleph, and Hazarmaveth, and Jerah,"

Almodad is possibly the founder of Arabia Felix (Yemen). His name might mean "immeasurable." In the Targum Pseudo Jonathon it is elucidated that he measured the earth with cords. Sheleph means "a drawing forth." He has been rather positively identified in a region of Southern Arabia and also Yemen. Hazarmaveth means "dwelling of death," quite possibly. Hadramaut on the Indian Ocean is supposed to be a positive identifier of the descendants of Hazarmaveth. Jerah means "the moon," or "smelling sweet," and is again associated with Southern Arabia.

Genesis 10:27 "And Hadoram, and Uzal, and Diklah,"

Hadoram means "noble honor" or "the south." He inhabited modern Yemen. Uzal means I shall be flooded. Was Joktan concerned about another flood? Uzal evidently inhabited Sanaa in Yemen. Diklah means "palm grove," and besides being in Arabia, the location is uncertain.

Genesis 10:28 "And Obal, and Abimael, and Sheba,"

Obal, the eighth son of Joktan means "stripped bare." His locale is uncertain. Abimael means "my father is God (El)." Some speculate his was a nomadic tribe near Mecca. Sheba was also the name of a son of Cush. His name means "seven" or "an oath." Multiple locations bear this name, in Arabia and Ethiopia. The most likely designation is Southern Arabia.

Genesis 10:29 "And Ophir, and Havilah, and Jobab: all these were the sons of Joktan."

Ophir is mentioned 13 times in Scripture and is often associated with gold. It means "reducing to ashes," and of the various locales mentioned in Scripture, the one mentioned here seems to be Southern

Arabia. Havilah means "circle," and is mentioned in the Edenic world of Chapter 2, and also as a son of Cush. This particular Havilah is likely somewhere in Arabia. Jobab, some have equated with Job. His name means "a desert," or "a place of crying out," or "where wild animals cry." Some feel it was an Arabian tribe near the Indian Ocean.

It is mentioned that all of the 13 were sons of Joktan, but not that they were all of his sons. And as is usually the case, the daughters, if any, are not mentioned. This possibly goes back to 5:2.

Genesis 10:30 "And their dwelling was from Mesha, as thou goest unto Sephar a mount of the east."

Mesha means "freedom," and is associated with the port city of Maushid in Western Arabia. Sephar means "numbering," and is found in Southern Arabia. So, a goodly portion of Arabia, especially in the south, and Yemen, were the settlements of the sons of Joktan.

Genesis 10:31 "These are the sons of Shem, after their families, after their tongues, in their lands, after their nations."

Japheth's genealogy was in four Verses, Ham's in 15 Verses, and Shem's in 11. We notice again that it is families, then tongues (indicating after the Tower of Babel), their lands (which indicates private property ownership, under God, of course), and their nations (which indicates some type of organization and authority structure, as well as laws).

Genesis 10:32 "These are the families of the sons of Noah, after their generations, in their nations: and by these were the nations divided in the earth after the flood."

In this Verse we have a kaleidoscopic view of the next period of time, and in some cases until the coming of the LORD some 4,000+ years later. Notice as well, Nations are God's idea, and lucifer is the one who is seen to weaken the Nations in Isaiah 14.

Chapter 11

IN CHAPTER 11 WE HAVE two main events: The Tower of Babel with its subsequent confusion of tongues and the scattering of Noah's offspring, and also the lineage of Abram. The line of Abram is also the Messiah's line. Chapter 11 functions much like Chapter 5, in that Chapter 5 was bringing us to Noah, a righteous seed. And Chapter 11 is bringing us to Abram, the founder of the Hebrew Nation, and the lineage of Messiah Jesus. Some would include a similarity to the generations of Adam here as well, in Chapters 1-2, showing us the founder of the human race.

Genesis 11:1 "And the whole earth was of one language, and of one speech."

This is saying that not only did the entire earth have one language, but they also had one dialect. The language did not have subsets to it. This is also an example of the Hebrew word for "one," "echad," being synonymous with "yacheed," as an absolute one, and not a compound one. Many try to say echad always has a compound unity connotation, but it is clear throughout Scripture that is not the case. Context shows whether it is singular or plural.

Mankind was unified. The unspoken backdrop here is that Nimrod was in the midst of the unified people stirring yet more rebellion against God, barely a century after the Flood.

Genesis 11:2 "And it came to pass, as they journeyed from the east, that they found a plain in the land of Shinar; and they dwelt there."

The "they" seems to refer back to the whole earth. Noah? Shem? Be that as it may, over the course of time, somehow they made their way past Mesopotamia, and then began migrating back. This Verse is a reason some feel that Noah's Ark and Ararat must be in Iran, or somewhere on the West side of Shinar. But it could just be migration, looking for the best place to settle in the reformed earth. Exploration of the post-Flood world would have been natural.

Shinar means "the land between two rivers." It would have been a rich, alluvial plain, and at that time near the tip of the Persian Gulf. An ideal place to settle. With the glaciers from the ice age receding, but still much farther south than the current icecap, the weather would have been idyllic as well. A great location.

Genesis 11:3 "And they said one to another, Go to, let us make brick, and burn them throughly. And they had brick for stone, and slime had they for morter."

So, instead of continuing their migration, they now begin to settle down. In Genesis 9:1 they were told to replenish the earth. But they were not spreading out. Hard brick and slime would do for brick and mortar in building. The fabulous walls of Ur, Ziggurats, among other finds of archaeology, show how amazing the building process became in a short period of time after the Flood. This very well could have been the first time for making brick after the Flood if they were migratory. The eight souls on the ark would have had access to the remembrance of antediluvian technology, which very well could have been vast. Solomon says there is nothing new under the sun.

Ussher, with some historical support, says the events of the Tower of Babel saga occurred in 2242 BC. It has been my experience when secular history contradicts Biblical history, the Bible is correct. So often the speculations of secular history vacillate, and true evidence points back toward the Biblical account.

Genesis 11:4 "And they said, Go to, let us build us a city and a tower, whose top may reach unto heaven; and let us make us a name, lest we be scattered abroad upon the face of the whole earth."

This is one of the more disputed Passages in Scripture. Many feel the proper translation should indicate a tower with heaven at the top, i.e., that the constellations and possibly astrology would be studied at the top. That the ancients had a keen eye toward the study of the heavens is confirmed by historical discoveries. The Great Pyramid, as well the as the various Henges (such as Stonehenge) throughout the world show great astronomical alignment. It is said the Egyptians knew the path of the North Star 25,000 years into the future. We know the Babylonians practiced trigonometry, and even had a sexigismal system that is still the elementary rubric of computer science.

I would be inclined to say the translation here is correct. It seems they were fearful of another Flood. Build a city above the clouds, and we have no worries. Notice as well this is done in rebellion. It says, "lest we be scattered abroad upon the face of the whole earth." But God told them to be fruitful and multiply and replenish the earth (Genesis 9:1). So the mob went against God. Build a city, and a tower. Much has been written about the Tower of Babel and archaeology. A few different possibilities are extant, as are mentions in antiquity. I would refer you to the Archaeology of the Premier Study Bible and also Holden and Geisler's book on Archaeology for a fuller elucidation of the evidence.

Genesis 11:5 "And the LORD came down to see the city and the tower, which the children of men builded."

Jehovah comes down to see what is happening. There is much to unpack here. If Jehovah is Omnipresent, why would He have to come down? Is Jehovah a demiurge or an emanation from God Elohim? Is this speaking of the angel with God's Name in it (Exodus 23:21)? Or the Angel of His Presence (Isaiah 63:9)? Or are there multiple Jehovah's, as some attest? The Bible does mention Seven Spirits of

God. It could be figurative language that God just began to pay closer attention or focused on the things on earth, as opposed to the things in Heaven. But one would assume God being God, He could focus everywhere equally. But He does have to humble Himself to behold the things in Heaven and earth (Psalms 113:6). It could also mean that He came as a Theophany, or a visible appearance of the Invisible God. He may have even appeared to the populace as such. I have no doubts God knew what they were doing, as He is Omnipresent.

Genesis 11:6 "And the LORD said, Behold, the people is one, and they have all one language; and this they begin to do: and now nothing will be restrained from them, which they have imagined to do."

God speaks as He did to Noah in Genesis 9, and so often before. Who is He speaking to here? Generally, or to angels, or to all throughout time in Scripture? And what He says is an amazing attestation to the power of unity. The people is (not are, showing their intense unity) in purpose. There was no deviation. There was no communication barrier. They will succeed in their task. Their ingenuity, brains, focus, will allow them, not to make it to the Third Heaven of course, but well into the atmosphere. Even in rebellion, they were going to accomplish their task of a city and a tower.

Many see similarities here between Babel, and the Babylon of Revelation 17-18 when the world will be as one. Once again in rebellion.

Genesis 11:7 "Go to, let us go down, and there confound their language, that they may not understand one another's speech."

Here we find that Jehovah was speaking possibly to the angelic realm. Notice He was here (Verse 5), but also able to talk to the angels in Heaven. To go down is the phraseology, indicating they were located up. He could have been taking counsel with His own will (Ephesians 1:11). But that seems not to be the case. And the goal was to confound man's language. Historical linguists find it unusual that man's language is devolving. It was more complex 4,000 years ago than today. It is very difficult to explain from an evolutionary paradigm. The multiplicity of languages appearing fully developed is also a perplexity for evolution.

Notice confounding speech would cause disunity.

Genesis 11:8 "So the LORD scattered them abroad from thence upon the face of all the earth: and they left off to build the city."

There is only One Jehovah (Deuteronomy 6:4 being a key cornerstone of Biblical Theology), so the "us" in 11:7 must not be speaking of two Jehovah's. In 3:22 we saw that Jehovah was speaking to Cherubim. It is likely He was including the Heavenly Council in this as well, such as Watchers, and the like. Remember in Daniel the Watchers were actually allowed to make decisions for things on earth under God, of course. Here, He could have been speaking to an Angel with His Name in it, or His Presence, as well.

We also have the fact of just how did the LORD scatter them abroad? Did He supernaturally transport them to the farthest regions, or did they just scatter, once the ability to communicate was gone? It would seem plausible that once their languages were confounded, the ones that could speak the same language would tend to stay together. There are certain historical references to this event, that are dealt with in other sources. This is by far the best explanation for the origin of multiple languages that has been postulated. Why would people in similar climes and circumstances develop an entirely different language from people a few hundred miles away, or in some cases just a few miles away? And how did these languages appear simultaneously, fully functional?

Genesis 11:9 "Therefore is the name of it called Babel; because the LORD did there confound the language of all the earth: and from thence did the LORD scatter them abroad upon the face of all the earth."

Babel means "confusing," or "mixing." We still refer to someone babbling. Possibly this is where the term "baby" came from, since babies cannot fully articulate their words to communicate. Most people feel this is the basis of Babylon, but some dispute this designation. I think Babel is the foundation for Babylon. Zephaniah 3:9 offers an interesting Scripture of the future when it says, "For then will I turn to the people a pure language, that they may all call upon the name of the LORD, to serve him with one consent."

Some feel the mouth of the lion in Revelation 13 refers to the English language, as Brittania has been symbolized as a lion.

Mankind now obeys, though unwilling. Every knee shall bow and every tongue shall confess that Jesus is Lord, only some will do so too late.

Genesis 11:10 "These are the generations of Shem: Shem was an hundred years old, and begat Arphaxad two years after the flood:"

Now we come to the second division of Chapter 11, the genealogy of Shem, which plays such an important role in human history. We find from this Passage Shem was 98 during the Flood. This Verse would have been approximately 2346 BC or 1658 Anno Mundi. Some think Arphaxad means "I shall fail at the breast," or "he cursed the breast bottle." Possibly he drank cow or goat's milk, or something else other than his mother's milk, if that meaning of his name is correct.

Genesis 11:11 "And Shem lived after he begat Arphaxad five hundred years, and begat sons and daughters."

So, Shem had other unnamed sons and daughters, just as Chapter 5's genealogy said of its constituents. I will at this time give some interesting material from the Reese Chronological Study Bible concerning dates and ages about this time period. The validity of the said dates is up to the reader to decide.

Reese lists the age of Nimrod at the Tower of Babel at 69, and Noah would have been 706. He says Nimrod would have founded Babylon at age 77, and began his kingdom at 129. Mizraim would have founded Egypt when he was 158, and Ham 258.

Another interesting thing is that Shem would have died around 1846 BC. He would have been a contemporary with Abraham for 150 years, and Isaac for 50 years. Shem would have been contemporary with Methuselah before the Flood for 98 years, and Methuselah would have been contemporaneous with Adam for over 200 years. Think about that. Adam-Methuselah-Shem-Isaac, from The Garden of Eden to 500 years after the Flood, with many decades to discuss things. Only four generations separated the Garden with Isaac. It is at least suppositional that truth would have been preserved, and what life would have been like in Eden could have been discussed. And what was expected of man as a result. As an aside, some think that Shem was Melchizedek.

Genesis 11:12 "And Arphaxad lived five and thirty years, and begat Salah:"

Shem would have been 135. Noah 737. Many of these descendants we discussed in Chapter 10. Salah may mean "sprout." This would have been about 2311 BC.

Genesis 11:13 "And Arphaxad lived after he begat Salah four hundred and three years, and begat sons and daughters."

Arphaxad would have died at around 1908 BC, or when Abraham was 88. Shem would have been about 538 when he died, and Ishmael about 3.

Arphaxad also begat sons and daughters. Fruitful and multiplying. Probably no birth control. The earth would be rapidly populating.

Genesis 11:14 "And Salah lived thirty years, and begat Eber:"

This would have been about 2281 BC. Eber means "the region beyond." It appears there are five people in Scripture with this name. We have already discussed the probability of the term "Hebrew" being a derivative of this name.

Genesis 11:15 "And Salah lived after he begat Eber four hundred and three years, and begat sons and daughters."

Salah, just like his father, live 403 years after the birth of his firstborn (it is assumed it is the firstborn). He would have died around 1878 BC. Abraham would have been around 118 and Shem would have been approximately 568.

Genesis 11:16 "And Eber lived four and thirty years, and begat Peleg:"

Peleg means "division." Ussher says, on page 22 of the "Annals of the World," The Tower of Babel happened five years after the birth of Peleg, according to Georgiius Syncellus' translation of the "Book of Sothis." (Manetho Book of Sothis 1. 1. 1:239) – the parenthetical supplied by the Editors of the Master Books edition of Ussher's work. This would have been around 2247 (Peleg's birth). Ussher also supplies a reference from the Apocrypha, Wisdom 10:5, which refers to the conspiring of the people to hinder the dispersion.

Shem would have been 199 years old when Peleg was born. Noah 801. However the earth was divided, it was in the days of Peleg. That may not necessarily mean the day of his birth.

Genesis 11:17 "And Eber lived after he begat Peleg four hundred and thirty years, and begat sons and daughters."

As Ussher says, Heber, the fifth from Noah…lived the longest of any who were born after the flood. He outlived Abraham… Abraham would have died in 1821 BC. Eber in 1817 BC. Isaac would have been 79 when Eber died, Ishmael 94 years old, and Jacob and Esau 19 years old. Easily, Jacob and Esau could have known a man that lived coterminous with Noah for 283 years. Again, we see the begetting of sons and daughters.

Genesis 11:18 "And Peleg lived thirty years, and begat Reu:"

Arphaxad was 35 when his son Salah was born. Salah was 30, Eber was 34, Peleg was 30, Reu 32, Serug 30, and Nahor 29 years when it was recorded they begat their (assumed) firstborn sons. Reu means "friend." Reu would have been born in 2217 BC. Shem would have been 229, and Noah 831.

Peleg lived. Everyday life continued. It is so easy to skip over these genealogical portions, and not realize that days, weeks, months, and years went by in the mundanity of life. Whatever living consists of, or consisted of, Peleg, and the other peoples, experienced it. The pains, joys, and sorrows of everyday existence. What it means to be human.

Genesis 11:19 "And Peleg lived after he begat Reu two hundred and nine years, and begat sons and daughters."

Peleg died at 239 years of age. He is the first recorded to have a dramatically shorter lifespan after the Flood. Entropy was closing in. The effects of the Fall of man, coupled with the less idyllic conditions after the Deluge, were combining to shrink man's lifespan. Now of course, I am just assuming they died at this point, and that this is not just the time they ceased being fertile. But it is telling, possibly, that unlike the genealogies of Chapter 5, the phrase, "and he died," is absent. So it could very well be an assumption on my part, when that phrase is lacking, to say this is when the particular personages passed away. But in my mind, the phrase "lived after" serves the same purpose as he died. It is as if in Chapter 5 God was wanting the full force of the results of the Fall to hammer home in our human spirits. If it does mean he died, Peleg died before Noah, in 2008 BC, approximately. I did want to note, even when I fail to put a modifier such as approximately, etc. in these dates, it should still be assumed that there could be slight differences in these dates. Floyd Nolen Jones is also an excellent resource on this subject of Old Testament chronology.

Genesis 11:20 "And Reu lived two and thirty years, and begat Serug:"

Reu means "friend." Serug means "branch." In Luke 3:35 he is called Saruch. He would have been born about 2185 BC, 1819 AM, or 2529 Julian Period. Shem would have been about 261 years old, and Noah about 863.

Genesis 11:21 "And Reu lived after he begat Serug two hundred and seven years, and begat sons and daughters."

Again, we see a dramatic shortening of age. Reu, like Peleg his father, lived to be 239 years old. Reu, the seventh from Noah, would have died about 1978 BC. Sarai would have been about 8 years old, Abram 18. Beginning in 1894 BC Apophis would have reigned in Egypt 61 years, and after him Jannas ruled Egypt for 50 years and 1 month, according to Ussher. Noah would have died 20 years before Reu, Shem 132 years later than Reu.

We do not necessarily know who his sons and daughters were, other than certain identifications and affiliations found in the commentary on Chapter 10.

Genesis 11:22 "And Serug lived thirty years, and begat Nahor:"

Serug was the eight from Noah, and Nahor the ninth. Nahor would be Abram's grandfather. Nahor means "snorting." The Rabbi's speak of the Divine snorting's of God. According to their tradition, you could hear God's snorting's on the Ark of the Covenant. We are in the image of God, and since we breathe, so the reasoning goes, so does God. Randall Price goes into this in one of his popular books on archaeology. Getting back to Nahor, he would also have a grandson named after him. Nahor, son of Serug, would have been born about 2155 BC.

Genesis 11:23 "And Serug lived after he begat Nahor two hundred years, and begat sons and daughters."

Serug has the shortest lifespan yet in this genealogy, 230. Serug would have died about 1955 BC, when Shem would have been about 491 years old, Abram 41, and Sarai 31.

Genesis 11:24 "And Nahor lived nine and twenty years, and begat Terah"

Nahor was the youngest in this genealogy to begat a child, at age 29. Terah means "station" or "delay." Joshua 24:2 gives some interesting information concerning Terah. It reads, "And Joshua said unto all the people, Thus saith the LORD God of Israel, Your fathers dwelt on the other side of the flood in old time, even Terah, the father of Abraham, and the father of Nachor: and they served other gods."

The implication is that Terah, and quite possibly at least some of the lineage before him, worshipped other gods. The "they" in this Verse may be referring to Abraham and Nachor. There are many apocryphal tales of how Abram began to worship the One True and Living God, such as God appearing to him as he was worshipping in a pagan temple. Or that Abram clung fiercely to that belief against all odds. Did he confront Nimrod? We are not sure if they were congruent with one another. The reality of the matter is, we do not know about any of Abram's conversion experience, really.

Terah was born in 2126 BC. Noah would have been about 822 and Shem about 320.

Genesis 11:25 "And Nahor lived after he begat Terah an hundred and nineteen years, and begat sons and daughters."

Nahor dies at the age of 148, a lifespan 36% shorter than Serug.

Genesis 11:26 "And Terah lived seventy years, and begat Abram, Nahor, and Haran."

This reminds one of the birth of Noah's three sons. According to Ussher, Haran was the oldest of the three sons, and was born about 2056 BC. Abram would not be born until 60 years later in 1996 BC.

Abram means "high father." Nahor again means, "snorting." This is a different Nahor obviously, than the one mentioned above. Haran means "mountaineer," and is also the name of two others persons in Scripture, and the name of a major city in the ANE.

Genesis 11:27 "Now these are the generations of Terah: Terah begat Abram, Nahor, and Haran; and Haran begat Lot."

"These are the generations," or a similar phrase is used six times heretofore, 2:1, 5:1, 6:9, 10:1, 32, 11:10. As stated before, this is a natural division of the Book of Genesis, and some feel it was actually clay tablets on which the records were written, each tablet beginning with this phrase. Now we learn the origination of Abram's nephew Lot. Lot means "covering." From now through Chapter 24, the major focus will be on Abram/Abraham. It will cover approximately 175 years, or the lifespan of Abram/Abraham, while from Creation to this point covers over 2,000 years. The life of Abram/Abraham will actually cover more Chapters in Scripture than Creation, Eden, the Fall, Cain and Abel, the Flood, Babel, and the dispersion of Nations.

It has been pointed out that Genesis 1-11 speaks of four great events, Creation, The Fall, The Flood, and Babel. 12-50 speaks of four great people, Abraham, Isaac, Jacob, and Joseph. Abraham had I's (eyes) of faith, Ishmael and Isaac. Bruce Wilkinson in his great "Walk Thru the Bible" series gives us that, and so much more wonderful information on the Bible.

With this Verse, we begin to learn about this man of faith, Abraham, the friend of God. The New Testament begins with the generations of Jesus Christ, the son of David, the son of Abraham, in Matthew 1:1.

Genesis 11:28 "And Haran died before his father Terah in the land of his nativity, in Ur of the Chaldees."

We do not know when Haran died. We are also here introduced to Ur of the Chaldees for the first time. Ur means "light," and at least six cities in the ANE have been discovered with this name. The earliest and most famous is the one mentioned here, Abraham's home. I should mention, at times, before Abraham's name is changed from Abram, I will still use the name Abraham. Most of the time however, I will refer to Abram as just that, Abram, before his name is changed.

Ur is amazing in its archaeology and civilization. Nanna the moon god was its patron deity (interestingly enough in Akkadian nanna is called "sin." Some feel this is where the root for Sinai came from). Its first recorded king was Mesannepeda. In Abram's time it would have been a coastal city at the mouth of the Persian Gulf, near the head of the Euphrates River, but it is now inland. Its current name is "Tell el-Muqayyar" in Southern Iraq.

Incredibly, being at that time a coastal town, imports were coming from vast distances, showing the development of the ancient world. Thousands of cuneiform tablets have been uncovered detailing the entire array of civilization, from business, education, the home, and religion. Some of the more remarkable discoveries are the Standard of Ur Mosaic, showing the king with his armies, among other scenes. The Lizard Headed Nursing Woman, which is as curious as it is also the basis of unique interpretations and conspiracy theories. The Gold Helmet of the King of Ur portrays a high degree of metallurgy, design, and wealth.

So Haran passed away before Terah.

Genesis 11:29 "And Abram and Nahor took them wives: the name of Abram's wife was Sarai; and the name of Nahor's wife, Milcah, the daughter of Haran, the father of Milcah, and the father of Iscah."

Notice that Abram and Nahor took them wives, which may indicate some sort of patriarchal deal making, where the woman may have had little say in the matter. Or, it could be a turn of phrase indicating they got married. We know from other Passages of Scripture that while arranged marriages were seemingly prevalent, other forms picking a spouse, even women choosing, was not unheard of in Pentateuchal times.

Sarai means "princess." She, like Abram, will have her name changed as part of God's Covenant with them, just as our name is changed to the family name of Jesus in our Covenant with God (Ephesians 3:15 among others). Sarai is referred to by name 17 times in Scripture. We will discover later that she is Abram's half-sister.

We also find that Haran had two daughters, Milcah and Iscah. So Nahor married his niece. This was evidently allowed since the gene pool was so close to the disembarkment from the ark. Milcah means "queen." She is the grandmother of Rebekah, and some say she was Sarai's sister. Iscah means "one who looks forth." Some say Iscah is another name for Sarai, and indicates Sarai's role as a prophetess i.e., one who looks forth, or one who sees. This is the only mention of Iscah in Scripture. Some say this is the origination of the name "Jessica." One account I saw made a connection with this and a mention in Shakespeare's "Merchant of Venice," but I am not acquainted with the specific connotation.

Genesis 11:30 "But Sarai was barren; she had no child."

With the command to be fruitful and multiply, childlessness carried a stigma. Both the barren woman, and those acquainted with her would look on it with disapproval. This is the first mention of 23 of the word "barren" in Scripture.

Genesis 11:31 "And Terah took Abram his son, and Lot the son of Haran his son's son, and Sarai his daughter in law, his son Abram's wife; and they went forth with them from Ur of the Chaldees, to go into the land of Canaan; and they came unto Haran, and dwelt there."

Terah, being the Patriarch of the family, was the leader of the move, even If God had spoken to Abram to leave Ur. We may expound on this more later, but some see disobedience in Abram's taking Terah and Lot with him. Much notice is given to the fact Abram will not enter the Holy Land until Terah dies, and will get further promises from God once he separates from Lot. Lot's progeny would go on to be at enmity with Abram's promised seed.

   Terah's journey to Haran from Ur would be approximately 600 miles in a straight line. Ur would be about 50 miles South of Babylon. It is uncertain what year this journey took place. Possibly 1922 BC, but that would be the latest.

   Some items from Ussher would be in order here. Ussher quotes a historian who says that Ur was home of priests and mathematicians, who because of this were known as Chaldeans. This name would still be in use almost 1500 years later, in Daniel's time. Other, less corroborated material was likewise transmitted from this historian. Ussher would have put the date that Chedorlaomer, King of Elam, conquered the Pentapolis including Sodom and Gomorrah, and putting them under tribute, at 1925 BC.

Haran, being quite a bit older than Abram, must have left Ur earlier, and began this city, if indeed he is the founder of this city, and not another Haran. The reasoning may have been Ur (meaning "light"), was so corrupt with the worship of idols, Haran left going toward where the ark landed, which presumably would have been purer in worship with the influence of Noah. In the Epic of Gilgamesh, Utnapishtim seems to represent the Biblical Noah, and lived near this area. But these are suppositions about Haran, and not necessarily fact. But again, one can see the reasoning. If Haran was Terah's son, this area would be filled with his relatives.

Genesis 11:32 "And the days of Terah were two hundred and five years: and Terah died in Haran."

Terah would have died somewhere around 1922/21 BC, evidently, according to Ussher.

I did want to mention two quite unrelated things here, but that do pertain to discussions in the early part of Genesis. I would first of all like to mention the city of Adam mentioned in Joshua 3:16. In Book 1 of "Discussions in Scripture," I talked of various possibilities of where Adam was either created, or lived after his expulsion. I may have left out this possibility.

Secondly, and this would deal with Chapters 10 and the early part of Chapter 11 of Genesis, is, this Scripture, which I think is apropos. It is found in Deuteronomy 32:8, which reads "When the most High divided to the nations their inheritance, when he separated the sons of Adam, he set the bounds of the people according to the number of the children of Israel." God has always had His people in mind, even before they were a people, so to speak. But this Passage is of particular importance concerning Abram's journey to the Promised Land. As an aside, the term "Promised Land" is not mentioned in Scripture, and "Holy Land" is only mentioned once. But a careful study shows that both these terms are proper to be used, because several Scriptures convey these meanings, even without using the exact phraseology.

We once again come to the term "died." The Fall plagues mankind.

Chapter 12

WE NOW COME TO A PIVOTAL person in all of human history, Abraham, or Abram as he is called in the first part of our journey. Major religions of the world revere and honor him. We know where he is buried, in the Cave of the Patriarch's in Machpelah, modern Hebron. It is the second holiest site in Judaism, after the Temple Mount. One could argue that God goes into more detail concerning Abram/Abraham (I will from henceforth use either one or the other designation) than the great Apostle Peter. Paul, in Romans Chapter 4, Galatians 3 and 4, and Hebrews 11, among others Passages, goes into great detail about the life of Abraham. So, we enter this life in detail in Chapter12, approximately 1921 BC. He is 600 or so miles away from home. His father has just died, and he has his wife and nephew with him. And a call. A man of faith. Go where you have never been before, is his task. Through many trials, missteps, and great patience and faith, a seed, that will germinate and be fulfilled in Jesus Christ to save the world, will come from his dead loins. He will be known as an altar builder, friend of God, and intercessor. Let us look at this remarkable individual, and the people and events associated with his life.

Genesis 12:1 "Now the LORD had said unto Abram, Get thee out of thy country, and from thy kindred, and from thy father's house, unto a land that I will shew thee:"

"Had" is a key word here. It may strongly indicate that Jehovah (which I believe is preferable to Yahweh for many reasons), had spoken to Abram in Ur. Get out of Ur, and leave your kindred (relatives), and your father's house (Terah), and go by faith unto a land God will show him.

Notice: 1) It was personal. The call came to Abram. Just as God calls us as individuals. 2) Abram had to leave his family, as God calls us to leave and cleave to Him above our family (Luke 14:26). 3) Our heavenly country, which we have not seen, takes precedence over our earthly country.

Others see here God re-emphasizing His call that he gave to Abram in Ur. But Abram left, not knowing where He was going. He just knew there was a city whose Builder and Maker was God.

Leaving filial relationships is many times the most difficult part of coming to Jesus. Traditions and customs can hinder us. Jesus called His disciples to leave family and follow Him. We must be willing to do the same. It seems as if it is a covenant qualification. That is not to say that our families may not come in part or whole to Jesus, however. There are rather numerous instances of this happening in Scripture.

Truly Abram was a man of faith. And his family is to be commended for following him.

Genesis 12:2 "And I will make of thee a great nation, and I will bless thee, and make thy name great; and thou shalt be a blessing:"

The promise from God is startling. I will make of thee (singular) a great nation. At 75 years of age, he was childless, and Sarai's womb was dead according to Paul. God promised to bless Abram. Blessing began as mentioned in Scripture in Genesis 1:22. Noah and his sons were blessed in Genesis 9:1. Now God says he will bless Abram.

Blessing has a connotation of increase and multiplication. Abram believed God, and it was counted unto him for righteousness. He believed God by obeying Him, and leaving Ur, and going to the Promised Land.

Though Abram eventually had many offspring, God is here talking about a particular nation, Israel, and then the Church (Galatians 3:7). Both Israel and the Church are to be a holy nation. Also, He says He will make Abraham's name great. Not only will He change Abram's name to "father of a multitude," but billions around the world still claim a physical and spiritual lineage to Abraham.

He then says Abraham will be a blessing. How? Through Abraham's seed, the Word of God was given and established, at least in the Old Testament. Jesus was of the seed of Abraham, and of course, through Him, the entire Universe is blessed for eternity.

Notice as well it is God who makes, not Abraham's ingenuity, cunning, or planning. And Abram was blessed to be a blessing. Our obedience to God blesses others.

Genesis 12:3 "And I will bless them that bless thee, and curse him that curseth thee: and in thee shall all families of the earth be blessed."

A great nation, a great name, but the promises of God keep on coming. If people blessed Abraham, they would be blessed. If people cursed Abraham, they would be cursed. But in Abraham, all the families of the earth will be blessed. How? Through Jesus Christ, the Messiah. Through the Bible. God's light would shine to all. Abram came from light, Ur. But all the earth would be blessed with God's Spiritual Light through Abraham. It would be difficult to bless any person greater than Abraham was blessed. Even the doors of the New Jerusalem are graced with the names of his descendants.

Many operate under the assumption that the blessing and cursing extends to Abraham's seed as well. The terminology used is singular, however. But just as Levi was in the loins of Abraham according to Hebrews, a similar concept could apply here. American foreign policy has even been shaped by this promise in some instances. The blessing and cursing certainly played a role in the life of Abraham. I would think it still holds true today.

Genesis 12:4 "So Abram departed, as the LORD had spoken unto him; and Lot went with him: and Abram was seventy and five years old when he departed out of Haran."

Taking Lot with him would seem to violate the spirit of Verse 1. But Abram being obedient to God's Word, at least in departing from Haran and going by faith to a place he'd never seen before is indicative of the faith of faithful Abram.

We are not sure of the exact size of his party and wealth when he left Haran. But very soon thereafter, he was fabulously wealthy, and continued to increase seemingly throughout his life. The blessing was certainly upon him.

Genesis 12:5 "And Abram took Sarai his wife, and Lot his brother's son, and all their substance that they had gathered, and the souls that they had gotten in Haran; and they went forth to go into the land of Canaan; and into the land of Canaan they came."

Cursed Canaan. Several generations had been born since the cursing of Canaan, about 420 years before. Some would say Abram's journey was approximately 409 miles, depending on where one places Haran. They had gotten servants, here called souls. They also had substance. They gathered the substance. We are not entirely sure by what means it was acquired. As far as dangers on the journey, it would be assumed there would be robbers then as now. We do know over the course of a very short time, Abram had 318 fighting men. So his entourage could have been very substantial. Just to feed and have water and provisions on a daily basis for such a large multitude would have been quite an undertaking. Most likely, this was an enormous caravan on a fairly, well-traveled trade route between Egypt and Mesopotamia. God was protecting them.

Genesis 12:6 "And Abram passed through the land unto the place of Sichem, unto the plain of Moreh. And the Canaanite was then in the land."

The Canaanite was in the land. The descendants of Canaan would grow very debauched. There was already much immorality in the land at this time. Sichem means "shoulder," or "saddle," and would have been located directly below Mt. Gerizim. Moreh means "hill of the teacher." It is in Northern Israel.

The Ras Shamra Tablets and the Ebla Tablets have given archaeologists a detailed look at early Canaanite religion. Dozens of false deities are mentioned. Baal and Asherah are two of the chief deities, and many trace their beginnings back to Nimrod and his wife Astarte. The religion is confirmed to have been debased and vile.

The descriptions of the geography and people mentioned here have been confirmed by archaeology.

Genesis 12:7 "And the LORD appeared unto Abram, and said, Unto thy seed will I give this land: and there builded he an altar unto the LORD, who appeared unto him."

This is the first mention of Jehovah appearing to Abram. He had previously spoken to him. It was as if God was telling Abram this was the place of promise. This was also Abram's first altar he built to God recorded. God is invisible. This must have been a Theophany, or a visible representation of the invisible God.

If Canaanites were debauched, this is like Abram staking a claim of the land for Jehovah. Truth has to begin somewhere. In the New Testament, it began in the Upper Room, and spread throughout the world. Of what type altar Abram built, such as size and materials used, we have no indication. Whether Abram sacrificed there, as Noah did on his altar, we are likewise not told. This would not be Abram's last visitation from God nor the last altar he would build.

Genesis 12:8 "And he removed from thence unto a mountain on the east of Bethel, and pitched his tent, having Bethel on the west,

and Hai on the east: and there he builded an altar unto the LORD, and called upon the name of the LORD."

Bethel means "house of God." Hai, later called "Ai" was toward the East. Abram builds yet another altar to God. This is why Abram is sometimes called "the altar builder." This time we are told he called upon the name of the LORD, as the Antediluvians did in Genesis 4:26.

Many make a significance that the name Jehovah is used here, and not El or Elohim. Jehovah sometimes is referred to as God's covenant Name. Jesus is Jehovah Salvation. In Exodus we find Abram did not know the full signification of Jehovah. It reads, "And I appeared unto Abraham, unto Isaac, and unto Jacob, by the name of God Almighty, but by my name JEHOVAH was I not known to them." Exodus 6:3. In Genesis 17:1 God will appear as El Shaddai, or God Almighty. Almighty indicates only One. Jesus in Revelation is also called "the Almighty."

So Abram is living a nomadic life. He pitches his tent. Bedouins still roam these hills as they did 4,000 years ago. I have seen them. He built an altar either on or at the base of a mountain here. 2,000 years later, Jesus would die on a cross very near this same spot.

Genesis 12:9 "And Abram journeyed, going on still toward the south."

Abram continues going South, toward the Negev and Egypt. This is a very dry area. Provisions may have begun to get scarce for Abram's entourage, especially water. The famine, would of course, greatly exacerbate the conditions.

Genesis 12:10 "And there was a famine in the land: and Abram went down into Egypt to sojourn there; for the famine was grievous in the land."

Famine, or a lack of food hit Canaan. We are not told whether it was a punishment for their sins, or if it was just a natural famine. But it was grievous, or very bad in the land.

My Pastor, Samuel L. Latta would always say, "never go to Egypt during a famine." Abram picked up something there, Hagar, whose offspring has been a constant challenge to the Israelites. Later, going to Egypt will actually keep the descendants of Abraham alive. When famine hit in Isaac's time, God specifically told Isaac not to go to Egypt (26:2). Sojourn means "to visit for a time."

Genesis 12:11 "And it came to pass, when he was come near to enter into Egypt, that he said unto Sarai his wife, Behold now, I know that thou art a fair woman to look upon:"

Uniquely enough, beautiful women are an Old Testament theme. Sarai, Rebekah, Rachel, Ruth, Esther, Abishag, the Shulamite, Bathsheba, among others. In the New Testament, the Bride of Christ is supposed to be beautiful in holiness. 12:10 is the first mention of Egypt in Scripture. Egypt in Hebrew is "Mizraim," and means "land of the Copts," or "double straits." Multiple times in Scripture, such as Deuteronomy 4:12 and Jeremiah 11:4, Egypt is referred to as the "iron furnace." It is generally seen as a type of the world.

Sarai would have been about 65 years of age here. Even though the Patriarchs, with DNA closer to the Fall, were living longer than we do currently, to be considered beautiful or fair at that age would still be considered quite an accomplishment.

Genesis 12:12 "Therefore it shall come to pass, when the Egyptians shall see thee, that they shall say, This is his wife: and they will kill me, but they will save thee alive."

Abram had thought through the scenario in his mind. He made an assumption, but quite possibly on his knowledge of the Egyptians or human nature and civilization generally at that time, that the Egyptians would kill Abram to obtain Sarai. The man dying for the woman, culminating with Jesus dying for His Bride, seems also to be somewhat of a theme of Scripture. Abram is here making a deal with his wife.

Genesis 12:13 "Say, I pray thee, thou art my sister: that it may be well with me for thy sake; and my soul shall live because of thee."

This would not be the last time Abram would use this tactic. And there was a kernel of truth in this statement, for Sarai was Abram's half-sister. But what one generation does in moderation, the next generation does in excess, seems to be literally fulfilled in this case, with Isaac telling basically an outright lie about Rebekah (though she was a relative, and if Lot could be called a brother to Abram, while being his nephew, Rebekah could conceivably be called a sister to Isaac in the customs of the day. See Genesis 26:7 for the specifics of this episode).

Abram will live because of Sarai seemingly. Notice the entreaty, "I pray thee." He realized that between famine in the Promised Land, and death in Egypt, he needed to petition Sarai very respectfully in this matter. Sarai is considered an archetypical great wife in 1 Peter 3. But she is seen with normal desires and feelings throughout the narrative. "That it may be well with me for thy sake," indicates Abram was placing his life in Sarai's hands.

Genesis 12:14 "And it came to pass, that, when Abram was come into Egypt, the Egyptians beheld the woman that she was very fair."

Very fair is an apt description of this woman of obvious beauty. Notice the superficiality of looks to the Egyptians. Egyptians are known in archaeology as being a very vain people in certain segments of society. Especially those that were concerned worthy to have reliefs on the copious architectural remains of this ancient period. Look through a book on Egyptian archaeology, and it becomes apparent that looks played a very important role in those segments of society. For example, it is said that earrings became a status in Egypt, because it meant the person cared enough about beauty to bleed for it. Quantities of mascara have been found in Egypt. Egypt in Scripture is usually a type of the world or worldliness.

It seems as though the first part of Abram's suspicions are coming to pass.

Genesis 12:15 "The princes also of Pharaoh saw her, and commended her before Pharaoh: and the woman was taken into Pharaoh's house."

At this early stage of human government after the Flood, 429 years earlier, we see already a burgeoning population and human government. Shem was still alive. We are not sure of Ham and Japheth. Possibly they could see history repeating itself. Princes, then Pharaoh saw Sarai, and she was taken to Pharaoh's house. Notice, it possibly wasn't quite a palace yet. Governmental power would continue to grow and increase in its dynastic aspirations. Among Jews, there are the Noahide Laws that are prescriptions for righteous gentiles and gentile government. We, of course, have no way of knowing if Noah really prescribed this to be followed after the Flood.

So, Sarai and Abram are separated, while in yet another foreign land. They were very much sojourners in the initial years the Bible begins to describe them. And it is here we will leave them until, God willing, Volume Three of Discussions in Scripture is available.

Discussions Two began with the Flood destroying the world. It ends with the hope of the world, literally, in Egypt, away from the Land of Promise, and the two who had the promise separated from each other, with only God as a way out. It was a seemingly impossible situation without God's intervention. Sarai, the mother of promise, in Pharaoh's house, one of the most powerful men on the planet, who even in this early stage, may have been equated with deity. Yet God will come through. God bless!

P.S. I have to say, I am indebted to Blue Letter Bible and Wikipedia for immense help, among other sources for this Commentary. Ussher is, in some ways, the foundation of the Commentary on the Scriptural Text, specifically in chronology and history.

www.ingramcontent.com/pod-product-compliance
Lightning Source LLC
Chambersburg PA
CBHW030200100526
44592CB00009B/369